WALLS

Debora Robertson

conran
OCTOPUS

First published in 1996 by

Conran Octopus Limited

37 Shelton Street

London

WC2H 9HN

This edition first published 1998

Commissioning Editor: Denny Hemming

Senior Editor: Catriona Woodburn

Art Editor: Tony Seddon

Picture Researcher: Rachel Davies

Production Controller: Mano Mylvaganam

Designers: Isabel de Cordova, Amanda Lerwill

Artwork Visualizer: Jean Morley

Illustrator: Clare Melinsky

A catalogue record for this book is available
from the British Library.

ISBN 1 85029 976 5

Printed in China

CONTENTS

Getting started

Given the bewildering range of wall colours and coverings
now available – from sponging and stippling with paint
to timber and metal cladding – creating a wall treatment
that works visually while complementing your personal
style can seem a daunting task. But if you weigh up all
the options before you start, use your colours with
confidence, and consider what is practical as well as
eye-catching, choosing the perfect look for your home
can be not only rewarding but surprisingly trouble-free.

Walls almost always dominate the look of a room, so they are one of the most important aspects of decorating your home.

As we move away from the more showy and 'decorated' interiors of the 1980s and into a more organic, evolved and understated look, it is important to find a look that suits you perfectly. If this sounds like a difficult task, bear in mind that it is also immensely liberating. Quite literally, anything goes. If you wish to combine a Mediterranean sense of colour with your favourite primitive oil paintings and a collection of Chinese ceramics, you can. It is simply a question of balance.

But how do you choose a style when the choice of wall-coverings is simply so dazzling in its breadth and variety? Deciding on the final scheme is a source of enormous anguish to most home decorators. How many of us have considered fantastically colourful swatches of paint, paper and fabric for months, only in the end – out of fear, confusion and terror of blowing our budget – to plump for magnolia in a cowardly fashion? But choosing a colour scheme does not have to be such an ordeal or fraught with difficulties. Colour is the most wonderful tool; it literally transforms everything it touches. Whether you wish to create a sense of peace in a bedroom, or a sense of drama in a dining room, the colour of the walls will have a profound effect on the finished product. Start thinking of colour as your ally, rather than as a source of anxiety, and you are on your way to a wonderful decorating adventure.

Before you start, gather together lots of samples of wallpaper and paint. If possible, get into the habit of carrying around Polaroids, fabric and colour swatches so that, wherever you are, you can match things up.

If you are keen to use specialist paint techniques, try them out on sheets of lining paper first, in order both to perfect the technique and to get a realistic sense of the colour and effect you are going to achieve. You can also make up the paint, wallpaper, tile and fabric swatches you have collected into colour boards, just as a professional interior decorator would.

Ideally, you should pin these up in the room where you intend to use them and then live with them for as long as you can. You will be amazed to see how that terracotta can look cosy and warm in one room and yet can appear a cheap and nasty orange in another. This exercise also allows you to get a sense of how the different elements work together, and gives you some idea of the effect daylight has on colour. This exercise may initially require time and patience, but it is worth the wait and the effort as it means that you are more likely to avoid expensive mistakes and also – ultimately – to create a scheme you are happy to live with for a long time.

Old houses present particular challenges. Often, the desire to be historically correct can be overwhelming but today the trend is against the slavish imitation of historical styles. Houses should reflect the lives, passions and preoccupations of their owners, rather than recreating an uncomfortable museum or quaint period drama. It is a

▲ *The wall treatment invariably dominates the overall look of a room. In this instance, a fabulous mosaic inspired by the planets and stars demonstrates that, in a small space, a bold scheme allows you to keep the rest of the interior furnishing details simple.*

question of reaching a successful compromise between sensitivity to the quality of your surroundings and your desire for a workable, modern scheme. And remember, the use of colour in old houses was often much more vivid than fading interiors, pictures and samples of fabric now would lead us to believe.

Practically speaking, several factors determine what kind of wall treatment is right for your home: budget; decorative style; your own level of skill and/or willingness to experiment with new techniques; and finally, practicality.

Of all the materials available to you, paint is probably the most versatile. Certainly, it is ideal for the budget decorator. Its versatility and dramatic potential has endeared it to many people working within strict financial constraints.

Wallpaper is available in myriad styles and patterns. Whether you are after floral abundance or formal restraint, there is something for you. For those people who are hesitant about attempting paint techniques such as dragging or sponging, there are wallpapers which imitate these effects quite realistically. Papers can be combined with borders and friezes for additional dramatic effect. And if wallpapering frightens you, because you think it takes a high level of skill, developments in recent years should take away any residue of anxiety. For example, self-adhesive papers can be hung straight from the roll and, more to the point, repositioned instantly if you make a mistake.

There are several other options if you are feeling courageous and would like to try something a little more unusual, or something a little less conventional than paint and paper. Fabric makes a fantastic wall-covering, and wood or metal cladding on interior walls has been through something of a revival in recent years.

The key to success is to spend some time evaluating the options open to you before you start to make any major decisions. You must work out exactly what is going to look right for your space. After that, be bold, be brave, be prepared to experiment – and follow the correct techniques to get it right!

◀ *The wall treatment you choose should be in keeping with the room's other decorative and practical elements. Here, a rough plaster wall distressed in warm ochre perfectly complements the simple units and collection of rustic kitchen accessories.*

▲ *A sense of harmony is created in this peaceful bathroom by using simple, blue-stained timber on walls, floors and window. The staining, when teamed with a classic white suite and a Matisse-inspired motif, creates a chic rather than a rustic look.*

Paint

Paint has often been called the decorator's best friend.
Quite justifiably so, for not only is it the most versatile
and the least expensive wall treatment available, it can also
be used to create an enormous range of effects. Even a
novice can produce some dazzling wall treatments in a
relatively short period of time. It is also an enormously
liberating material to work with, because even if your
experiments go disastrously wrong, it is a relatively
inexpensive and quick exercise to paint over them.

Whether you are inclined towards a bold modern look, or a delicate, subdued scheme, you can create any effect with paint; practically anything is possible. Your best guide will undoubtedly be the room itself.

There are, of course, some things that you probably cannot change – short of a complete remodelling job. The room's proportions, and the size and position of windows and architectural details, are probable starting points when you are deciding how to tackle the space. If you have a small room, for example, a pale colour will give you a brighter, more airy look. But equally, you might like to go in the opposite direction and use dark colours to enhance or create a cosy or 'clubby' feeling.

However, there is little point in setting yourself an impossible task. You can only work against a room's natural inclination to a certain point – further than that, and it proves to be a frustrating, fruitless and expensive exercise. For instance, a dark, north-facing room can rarely be made to look bright and cheerful, whatever its proportions. Indeed, a chilly light on bright, jolly colours can even make them look harsh, dreary and depressing. It is always best – as with other aspects of decorating – to work with what you have, enhancing and developing it. It is probably better to choose dark colours such as terracotta, mossy green or midnight blue for a north-facing room and then enjoy the challenge of creating a rich, opulent scheme.

In a badly proportioned room, using the same colour throughout, on walls, ceiling, and even on the floor, will blur the confines of the space. But remember that you can also combine paint colours and finishes to great effect. So, in a small room, gloss paint will reflect the light and give a more spacious feel. And if a room seems too high for its dimensions, a dark, matt paint on the ceiling will 'lower' it, or alternatively, you could add a dado rail and paint the area beneath it in a darker colour than the rest of the walls. If your room has low ceilings, you can create a more lofty appearance by painting the walls with vertical stripes (see pages 26–27), or by making the ceiling either matt white or a paler colour than the rest of the walls.

Of course, there are many different paint effects you can use to disguise the room's less attractive features; but equally, they can be used simply to create a dramatic effect. *Trompe l'oeil* effects, for instance, can also be used to create architectural interest where once there was none – and at a fraction of the cost of the real thing.

These days, we have moved away from some of the showier effects of the 1980s, when many a decorative crime was committed in the name of sponging and marbling. The look now is more subtle; the colours are more subdued; and, ultimately, final appearances are more sophisticated. If you are a decorating novice, this trend actually works to your advantage, because if you are working with two different shades of cream, terracotta or grey, mistakes and irregularities will be less glaringly obvious than if your colours had been more strident, and your overall schemes altogether less subtle. The fact that more relaxed, distressed interiors are increasingly popular probably also works in your favour.

As well as the enormous variety of paint colours available, the kind of paint you choose will have a huge bearing on the look you eventually achieve. Some purists would never use anything except matt emulsion finish on the walls and eggshell on the woodwork, but gloss finishes have gone through something of a revival recently. Vinyl silk and gloss finishes are wonderful in areas such as halls, bathrooms and kitchens which receive a lot of wear, as scuff marks can simply be washed off. Remember not to ignore the possibilities of textured paint either, because this does not have to mean full-blown Artex: manufacturers have recently developed a new range of paints, designed to cover minor cracks and imperfections in walls and ceilings, while appearing only slightly more textured than traditional vinyl matt emulsion – useful and unobtrusively interesting.

Paint's possibilities are almost endless. Practically speaking, it is simply a question of finding a product that suits the surface you are decorating and creates the look you want.

◀ *In a small room where solid terracotta walls could be rather oppressive, the decorator has used a clever, if simple, technique. The walls are painted off-white and small pieces of masking tape are stuck in a random pattern on the wall. The walls are then colourwashed and the tape peeled off to reveal white space beneath.*

▲ *Different types of paint offer an almost endless range of decorating possibilities. In this instance, a monochrome scheme is given an unusual injection of humour with one wall coated in blackboard paint. It's such a good idea, there is no need to restrict it to the nursery.*

Directory of paint
Standard paints

Eggshell

Oil-based eggshell has a smooth, hard-wearing surface and a slight sheen. A more elegant finish for woodwork than gloss, it can also be used on furniture and interior walls and ceilings as it provides a resilient surface and wears beautifully. It is therefore good for heavy-duty areas such as halls, bathrooms and kitchens. Can also be used for paint effects. Drying time: 12–16 hours. Look out for quick-drying water-based eggshell; this gives the same effect but lives up to its name and dries in 2–4 hours. **1**

Enamel

Use on metalwork for best effect, including radiators.

Gloss

Shiny gloss paints are mostly oil-based, but water-based varieties are now available. Available in semi-gloss, gloss and high-gloss finishes. High-gloss paint shows every bump and surface flaw. Durable, chip-resistant, and easy to wipe clean, gloss paint can be used on woodwork, metalwork and walls; it can also be used on plastic without an undercoat. It is perfect for heavy-use areas: hallways, door and window frames, children's rooms, kitchens and exterior woodwork. Liquid gloss must be used over proprietary undercoat, whereas non-drip and self-undercoating versions do not need undercoats. Drying time: 12–16 hours. **3**

Kitchen/bathroom emulsion

A water-based paint containing fungicide, for areas that may become damp.

Limewash

See Whitewash.

Oil-based mid-sheen paint

Also known as semi-sheen or satin finish. Similar to eggshell but with a

less attractive finish, this paint has been adapted for faster application; some varieties need no undercoat, require only one coat, and are drip-resistant. Can be used on woodwork, window and door frames. Drying time: 2 hours.

Primer

Specially designed to seal bare surfaces and available in water- or oil-based versions, special primers should be used for wood, plaster and metal.

Quick-drying eggshell

See Eggshell, water-based (above).

Soft distemper

See Whitewash.

Solid emulsion

See also Vinyl matt and Vinyl silk emulsions (below). A thick type of paint that comes ready to use in its own tray. Its heavy consistency reduces the risk of drips and splatters and is therefore appropriate for use on walls and ceilings. Do not use on new plaster without primer.

Textured paint

A water-based paint that adds texture to plaster surfaces. Usually used on walls and ceilings, it is particularly useful for covering up minor imperfections and rough surfaces. Difficult to clean. Be warned too: it is extremely difficult to remove if you change your mind.

Undercoat

A thick, opaque paint that fills in small cracks and irregularities in the surface being painted. Matt, slightly chalky texture. Available in either oil-based or water-based versions. Easy to apply and though it comes in few colours, it can be easily tinted. Use on primed surfaces. Do not use on plastic or stainless steel. Not intended as a finish but sometimes used as such. In heavy-use areas, where it is likely to get scuffed, use a matt varnish to protect it. Drying time: 8–12 hours.

Flat oil paint

A smart, flat paint which is a great favourite with decorators as a finish, or thinned as a glaze. Obtainable only through specialist paint suppliers. Drying time: 6–12 hours.

Historic colours

Enjoying a huge revival, these paints are sometimes mixed by eye – even today – using traditional materials, recipes and techniques. They do provide a wonderful depth of colour and the range of colours available is surprisingly wide. As a concession to modernity, these paint ranges are often available in a variety of finishes: matt emulsion, flat oil, eggshell, gloss, exterior paint, distemper, floor paint.

Use a brush, rather than a roller or pad, for a truly authentic effect.

Metallic paints

Using metallic paints in interiors is becoming increasingly popular. Basic metallic paints are cheaper than gold leaf where cost is a factor, although the finish is not as lustrous. Hammer-finish paints provide a variegated texture. Metallic paints usually require proprietary primers and thinners; they give a better finish if sprayed rather than applied with a brush, although on smaller areas such as radiators they can be brushed on if preferred. **5**

Whitewash

Inexpensive matt paint with a soft, powdery finish. It is easy to make, using a combination of calcium carbonate powder, rabbit-skin glue (or PVA) and water.

Distemper (limewash) is the same, but the whitewash is mixed with powder pigment to tint it to the colour required. Experiment until you get the right consistency and colour. Because it cannot be cleaned, it may be short-lived; it can even be rubbed off with time. Remove before applying oil-based or emulsion paint. **2**

Vinyl silk emulsion

A water-based paint similar to vinyl matt emulsion, this silk emulsion has a slight sheen finish and is more durable. Best suited to walls, it is also a good base for decorative finishes, mixing well with stainers, powder colours and water-based artist's tube colours. Drying time: 2–4 hours.

Special paints

Buttermilk

One of the earliest domestic paints, buttermilk was used widely in early American interiors and is still good for creating an authentic country feel. Made from soaked, dry pigment, buttermilk and a small quantity of fungicide to prevent mould, it has a matt appearance. As inconsistencies in mixing show up more markedly in dark colours, it lends itself better to paler shades. **4**

Vinyl matt emulsion

A water-based paint with a flat finish. Easy to apply, vinyl matt emulsion gives good coverage, and is quick to use – and cheap. It should be used on walls and ceilings, and can be used for paint effects – thinned to create a wash, it provides a good base for stencilling; thickened with whiting, it has a textured effect. Can be used on new plaster (once thoroughly dried) or on rough, porous surfaces such as interior stone or brickwork. Not easy to wash clean. Drying time: approx. 4 hours.

Preparing the surface for painting

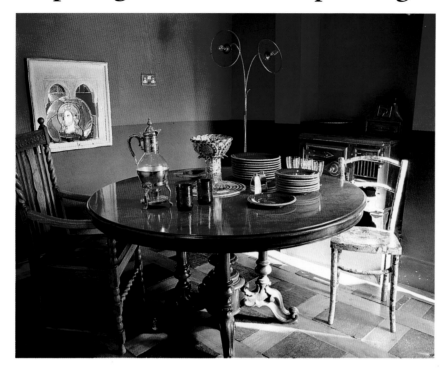

▲ *Paint is truly the simplest – and cheapest – way of making a decorating statement. Here, walls in blue and orange pick out colours from the stained glass window to stunning effect and require no further adornment. These colours are further reflected in the floor and interior furnishing.*

The quality of a paint finish is almost entirely dependent on thorough preparation. It is worth spending as much time as you can on this stage, in order to get it absolutely right.

A clean, smooth starting surface is essential to a smart finish. A good preparation will also make the application of paint easier, unless you want to achieve a 'distressed' effect (see pages 18–21). Invest in good-quality equipment – buy the best you can afford because it will last longer than cheaper alternatives.

Estimating quantities

The amount of paint you will need will depend upon the kind you are intending to use and the colour of the existing walls. For example, if you are painting dark green walls white, you will need more coats than if you were painting white walls dark green. If a wall has been replastered, bear in mind that new plaster will absorb more paint than old. The instructions on your tin of paint will give the amount of coverage you can expect from 1 litre (1¾pt) if you use it undiluted. This is sometimes called the 'spreading rate'. It is easy to work out how many square metres (yards) you have to cover. For the ceiling area, measure the length and width of the floor and multiply one measurement by the other. Calculate each wall separately: multiply the height by the width. Then add the wall areas together.

To calculate the amount of paint you will need, take the total area you are going to paint and divide it by the figure specified as the spreading area for 1sq m (1sq yd) on the tin. The result of this sum will be the number of litres (pints) of paint that you will need.

Preparing to paint

Before starting to paint, remove as much furniture as possible. Cover the remainder with dust sheets and the floor with plastic sheeting. Protect window frames with masking

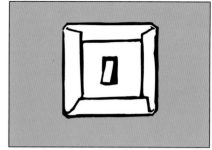

1 Protect light switches, electrical sockets and woodwork with strips of masking tape before you start.

2 Wash down the walls with a sponge and a solution of detergent.

3 Use a squeegee mop and a solution of detergent to wash the ceiling.

4 Before painting, prepare the surface, using a wide-bladed scraper to remove flaking paint.

Filling cracks

1 Use a filling knife or scraper to remove any debris from larger cracks.

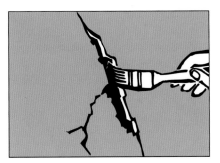

2 Remove any remaining dust with a soft-bristled paintbrush, or you could use a vacuum cleaner hose.

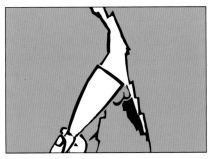

3 Fill the crack with a filling knife. Fill deep cracks in layers, allowing 24 hours' drying time between each.

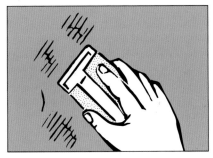

4 When the filler is dry, gently smooth the crack with a sheet of sandpaper wrapped around a sanding block.

tape. Cover anything you do not wish to paint, such as a radiator, with plastic sheeting, sticking it down with masking tape. Mask areas such as a ceiling with wide tape, if you are painting the walls, and vice versa. Assemble all the equipment you will need before you start and ensure that the room is ventilated. Wear overalls, but avoid woollens as fibres may stick to the paintwork.

Preparing the surface

Before painting a wall, you need to ensure that the plasterwork is in good condition; if it is not, it is essential that the old plasterwork is professionally removed and replaced before you begin. New plaster generally needs about four to five weeks to dry properly, so be sure to allow for this in your decorating schedule. It will then need a coat of plaster primer or thinned emulsion before being painted. New plasterboard walls require a coat of plasterboard primer-sealer or diluted PVA.

A previously painted wall should be thoroughly cleaned with strong detergent diluted in warm water. With walls, work from the bottom to the top, and pay particular attention to the areas around light switches where fingermarks accumulate. Wash ceilings using a clean squeegee floor mop. Rinse all surfaces with clean water. Allow to dry thoroughly before repairing minor defects in the walls. Remove flaking paint with a wide-bladed scraper. Then rub down walls with fine sandpaper to ensure a smooth finish, and dust off.

Treat any water stains or mould growth with proprietary stain blocks before you start.

Filling cracks

Any cracks should be filled with an interior filler. Using a scraper, first clean out the crack, removing any loose plaster or dust. Then, with an old paintbrush and clean water, dampen the crack and the surrounding area, so that it will bond well with the filler. Overfill the crack with all-purpose filler. Large holes can be built up in layers, but you will need to allow plenty of drying time between each one. Allow the filler to dry thoroughly and finally sand it smooth and level with the surrounding wall surface.

Tools and equipment

Have all the equipment you are likely to need to hand before you start, in order to minimize the time you spend preparing the wall or other surface to be painted. It is a good idea to put together a basic decorator's kit, rather as you would a family first-aid kit. This means that you are always equipped to tackle modest painting jobs, and only need add to it for more specialized tasks.

- **Sandpaper:** fine-grade glasspaper, wet-and-dry and coarser varieties, to key woodwork or smooth over repaired cracks.
- **Sanding blocks:** made of wood or cork, to wrap the sandpaper around.
- **Lint-free rags:** to wipe up spillages.
- **White spirit (also sold as turpentine):** solvent for oil-based paints.
- **Masking tape:** narrow tape to protect light switches, sockets, window panes etc, from paint; wide tape to mask off large areas such as edges of ceilings or walls.

- **Dust sheets:** either plastic or fabric.
- **Old spoon:** handle to be used to open pots of paint.
- **Scraper:** wide-bladed, to remove patches of flaking paint.
- **Filling knife:** to press filler into holes and cracks.
- **Wooden dowel:** to mix paint.
- **Sugar soap or household detergent:** to clean down walls prior to painting.
- **Interior or all-purpose filler:** to fill cracks or holes in walls.
- **Large decorator's sponges:** to wash down walls.
- **Clean glass jars:** to soak brushes, store small quantities of paint and numerous other uses.
- **Face mask, eye protection and disposable gloves:** essential when working with solvents and other harsh decorating materials.
- **Painting platform:** for reaching high ceilings and painting in hallways.

Using brushes, rollers and pads

▶ *Walls painted in contrasting solid blocks of colour have immense visual impact. When using solid colour, however, the finish needs to be immaculate, making it imperative that the surface preparation is thorough. Large expanses of wall without obstacles to paint around perfectly suit use of a roller and paint tray.*

duty industrial equipment unless you are renovating a whole house from top to bottom. If you require any expensive or specialized tools, consider hiring them instead.

First steps to painting walls

Before you start, dust the rim of the paint can with a dry brush or damp cloth to remove any dust or grit which could fall into the paint and contaminate it. Work your way around the tin with the spoon handle, levering gently until the lid flips off. Stir the paint thoroughly in a figure-of-eight movement with a clean piece of dowel.

Pour a quantity of the paint into a clean paint kettle, tray or plastic bucket because, when you are moving up and down ladders, this is easier to handle than a full tin.

Using a brush

Before using a new brush, get rid of loose bristles by working it vigorously backwards and forwards across the palm of your hand.

To begin painting, dip the brush into the kettle until one third to half of the bristles is covered. Remove the excess by dabbing the brush against the inside of the kettle, not by scraping the brush against the rim of the tin. Scraping it pulls the bristles out of the brush, contaminates the paint with stray bristles, and can make a mess of the outside of the tin. Alternatively, you could tie a piece of string taut across the top of the kettle and clean the brush against that. Do not be tempted to overload the brush as it will be much more difficult to manoeuvre and it will almost certainly result in drips that will show on the finished paint surface. It is also essential not to apply the paint too thickly and that you leave enough drying time between coats; consult the directions.

If you are using emulsion paint, you need to work fast because the rapid drying time of the paint can lead to shading. Using a 10–15cm (4–6in) brush, work across the room in areas approximately 70cm (28in) square. Use criss-cross brush-strokes to cover the area evenly and finish on a light, upward stroke. This is called 'laying off'. Move swiftly and methodically as you paint across the wall.

Brushes, rollers and pads

Make sure that you have the correct equipment for both the material you are using and the surface being painted in order to minimize the time the task will take. Never use brushes, rollers and pads that are past their best; the end product will not reflect the amount of time you have invested.

Good brushes have a decent length of bristle; they should not be stubby. Rollers can be more messy than brushes, as the paint is more likely to splatter, but they are a good choice for large areas such as walls and ceilings because they speed up the application.

Rollers produce a slightly more mottled surface than brushes. Indeed, if you want a super-smooth surface, do not use a foam roller, because the air trapped in the foam will produce an 'orange-peel' effect. And this texture will survive subsequent paint layers.

Paint pads are similar to rollers; using a paint pad is an excellent and speedy way of covering large surfaces. Made from mohair bonded onto a foam backing, they are available in several sizes. There are special edging pads for precision painting and small pads to use on mouldings and glazing bars. Best used with water-based paint, paint pads produce a smooth finish, but they do apply less paint per coat than rollers, so you may need an extra coat for the same density of finish.

Buy enough of the appropriate paintbrushes, rollers and paint pads for the task, but it is probably not worth buying heavy-

Handling the tools

1 When completing an area of painting, and before reloading a brush, finish with a light upward stroke.

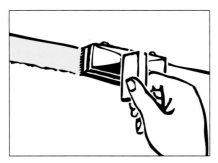

2 Use a small pad or special edging pad to go around the edges of the wall before you tackle the central area.

3 Apply the paint in overlapping criss-cross strokes working on an area of 1 sq m (1 sq yd) at a time.

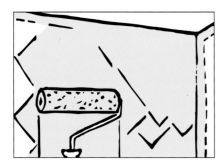

4 With a roller, apply the paint in overlapping criss-crosses followed by solid strokes.

Oil-based paint requires a different approach. It dries more slowly than emulsion and thus allows a little more flexibility. Use a smaller, 2.5–5cm (1–2in) brush, held between thumb and forefinger, like a pen, and begin to make parallel vertical lines of paint across an area measuring approx. 30 cm (12 in) square. When you have used up most of the paint on the brush, work swiftly across the vertical lines, blending them together into a solid layer of paint. Finish the area off with light, vertical strokes and move on quickly to the adjoining area.

Using a paint pad

Pour some well-mixed paint into a paint tray; you can use either a standard roller tray or one specially designed for use with pads. Load the paint by running the pad backwards and forwards over the ridged area of the paint tray, or over the loading roller in a paint-pad tray, to ensure an even application. Work on the edges of the wall first using a small pad or a special edging pad. Then, using a larger pad (approx. 20cm [8in] long is usually best), apply the paint in overlapping criss-cross strokes, working on an area of 1sq m (1sq yd) at a time. If you are painting ceilings or high walls, fitting the pad to an extension pole will speed up the process considerably.

Using a roller

Select a suitable sleeve for the wall surface and slide it onto the roller cage until it clicks shut. Pour some well-mixed paint into a roller tray and run the roller down the sloping part of the tray into the paint. Roll it up and down along the ridged slope to remove excess paint.

After cutting in (see pages 16–17) with a paintbrush at the edges of the room, apply the paint in side-to-side, up-and-down strokes, spreading the paint evenly over areas approx. 60cm (24in) wide. Lay off on a light upward stroke before reloading for the next area, taking care to blend the edges of the two areas together. If you are working on a ceiling or on high walls, you may wish to add an extension pole to the roller.

For advice on patterned rollers and use of rollers with textured paint, see pages 26–27.

Tools and equipment

- **Containers:** for paintbrushes, use metal or plastic buckets; for rollers, plastic trays.
- **Decorating brushes:**
  10–12.5cm (4–5in) brushes for walls.
  2.5–5cm (1–2in) brushes for details.
  5–7.5cm (2–3in) brushes for 'cutting in' around the tops of walls.
  2.5cm (1in) brushes or angled-headed brushes for window frames.
  a selection of artist's brushes for details.
  5–10cm (2–4in) oval-headed brushes for applying varnish.
- **Roller cage:** can hold a variety of sleeves.
- **Roller sleeves:**
  short-pile mohair for applying silk emulsion.
  medium-pile sheepskin for matt emulsion.
  medium-long pile for textured surfaces.
  patterned foam rollers for dramatic effects.
- **Extension pole:** for pads and rollers, when painting high areas such as ceilings.
- **Radiator roller:** small roller on a long handle for reaching into the awkward space behind radiators.
- **Paint pads:** often have hollow handles so they can be used with an extension pole.
- **Mahl stick:** to steady your hand for details.
- **Stepladder or ladders:** to create a painting platform.
- **For decorative paint effects:**
  pieces of natural sponge.
  flogger: for dragging.
  dusting brush or specialist graining brush.
  selection of stencilling brushes.
  large stippling brush.
  softener brush: to soften brush marks.
  fitch brushes: for spattering and stippling.
  specialist rollers, rockers and combs.
  lint-free rags: for rag rolling.

Equipment to hire

- **Spray guns:** to cover large areas very quickly. Always wear a face mask.
- **Battery-powered paintbrushes and rollers:** the paint is pumped from an attached reservoir along a plastic tube.
- **Scaffold tower:** a safe platform if painting a very high room.

Applying paint

Sequence of painting a room

Professional decorators always paint a room in a particular order. They start with the ceiling. The walls are next; then the woodwork around doors and windows; then cornices and skirting board; and finally, the floor. This ensures that paint spattering down from the ceiling does not ruin newly painted walls. Cleaning off any paint that drips onto woodwork immediately is another tip. It is easier to remove when it is still wet.

Applying paint

Before covering the walls in swathes of colour, you need to give some attention to the smaller details to ensure a professional finish. It is very important to create a precise finish around doors, windows and light fittings, as well as ensuring a neat line between ceiling and wall, as these are junctions which you will notice every time you enter or leave the room, or open or shut a window. You

Order of painting

1 Professional painters paint a room in a particular order. Follow this order for a professional finish.

2 Paint walls and ceilings in strips – top to bottom for walls; for ceilings, in alternating directions.

need to use a technique called 'cutting in'. Using a small brush, 2.5–5cm (1–2in), pressed firmly against the wall surface so that the bristles are slightly splayed, paint a band of paint approx. 2.5cm (1in) wide into the internal corners, wall and ceiling angles and above the skirting board.

You will need to make a similar band around doors and windows. You can do this in the same way or use a slightly different technique which ensures a neater finish. Paint a series of small, horizontal strokes at right angles to the door or window frame. Join together with a steady, firm vertical stroke of the brush, easing the bristles of the brush tight against the wooden frame.

Paint the ceiling using a roller attached to an extension pole. Paint sections in strips, working from one side of the room to the other and back again, so that the direction of application alters with each strip. In order to give solid paint coverage, within each strip apply the paint as when using a roller on a wall: starting with overlapping criss-crosses and finishing with straight strokes. When painting walls, paint in strips from the top of the wall to the bottom, starting from the side of the wall closest to any natural light source. Having painted the walls and ceiling, you should turn your attention to the precision painting areas: the doors and window frames.

Painting plaster mouldings

Next item in the sequence is the plasterwork: mouldings such as cornices and ceiling roses.

Because of the porous nature of plaster, mouldings are particularly susceptible to staining caused by damp, mould, mineral salts and nicotine. You must ensure that these have been adequately dealt with, the surface made good and primed before you start repainting. Ask at your hardware store for suitable products to tackle specific problems.

Mouldings should be painted with small paintbrushes or artist's brushes, depending on their size and the amount of detail they entail. Start by using a 2.5cm (1in) brush to apply the base colour, ensuring that the bristles are gently splayed to create a neat outer edge. When this colour has dried, you may wish to pick out some of the detail in a

Applying paint

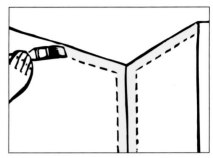

1 Before painting the wall, 'cut in' around the edges with a 2.5–5cm (1–2in) brush, with bristles slightly splayed.

2 Next, begin applying paint with a roller – in criss-cross followed by vertical strokes.

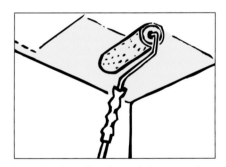

3 Paint the ceiling with a roller attached to an extension pole, working in alternating strips across the ceiling.

contrasting colour using a smaller artist's brush. If you are trying to paint a straight line or particularly fine detail, steady your hand by resting it against a mahl stick.

Painting metal pipes and radiators

Before you paint pipes or radiators, ensure that heating or hot-water appliances have been switched off. Check that the metal fixtures have had time to cool down. Ensure previously painted surfaces are free of dust by washing them down with a solution of household detergent. Key a high-gloss surface by rubbing down the paint with fine wet-and-dry paper. Rinse and ensure it is completely dry before starting to paint.

The longest-lasting finish for metal is created by using a proprietary metal or radiator paint or enamel. On radiators, use a 5cm (2in) brush and apply the paint as thinly as possible, working quickly with long, light strokes. Be very careful to avoid getting paint on or near the valves, as dried paint will cause them to stick. Use a small piece of card to prevent flicking paint onto the wall surface when you paint the edges of the radiator.

Pipes should be painted with the same paint as the radiator with a 2.5cm (1in) brush, working vertically from top to bottom.

Painting tiles

Applying paint to ceramic tiles is usually a short-term solution because, no matter how careful you are with preparation and application, paint will eventually chip or peel away from the glazed surface.

However, if you have a run of ugly tiles, giving them a quick coat of paint can act as a good facelift. Prepare the tiles for painting by washing them down with household detergent and a damp cloth.

It is now possible to purchase a proprietary tile primer which may prolong the life of a coat of paint. After this primer you should use two coats of gloss or enamel paint if you want a durable, waterproof finish.

◀ When painting details in contrasting colours, such as here on the wooden panelling and moulding, precision is essential. Use low-tack masking tape to define the areas to be painted. When painting on wood, first apply a primer and then an undercoat to ensure that a smooth, problem-free finish is achieved.

Painting other areas

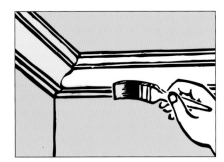

1 When painting details in contrasting colours, precision is essential. Use tape to mark off the areas to be painted.

2 Use a 2.5–5cm brush (1–2in) to paint radiators. Work quickly, applying the paint in a thin coat.

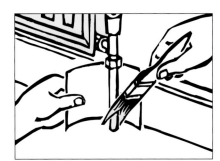

3 When painting pipes, use a piece of cardboard to prevent flicking paint onto the wall or skirting.

Paint effects guide

▲ *Oil glazes are a simple way to give walls a sophisticated sheen. When deciding on what colour to use and how much to tint the glaze, bear in mind that the colour will become noticeable quite quickly once on the walls. Here, a preliminary coat of pale yellow eggshell has been given greater depth and texture with a grey-tinted glaze.*

Using glazes

Possibly the simplest material for the amateur to master, a tinted oil glaze applied on a base coat will add a subtle layer of colour, softening it and giving it greater depth.

Walls need to be carefully prepared (see pages 12–13) and then coated with one or two layers of eggshell paint. Sometimes, it is possible to use emulsion and a water-thinned wash as an alternative to glaze. However, the finished effect is seldom as elegant as that produced by an oil-based finish.

You can prolong the life of the effect – whether oil or water-based – by applying a coat of matt varnish when it is thoroughly dry. This is very important if you have painted a heavy-traffic area such as a hallway, or if it is likely to need frequent sponging.

To apply, paint the glaze onto the wall with a medium-sized decorating brush, covering 1sq m (1sq yd) at a time, using quick, random strokes. Soften brushmarks with a wide, short-bristled brush, and continue until the surface is evened out, and until you have created a thin film of near-transparent colour.

Washes

Washes are made from water-based paint. They provide a soft finish but they are less flexible and less easy than glazes for the beginner because they dry quickly.

Washes are best applied over a matt emulsion base. For effects such as rag rolling, the wash needs to comprise 1 part emulsion to 3–5 parts water. For colourwashing, it needs to be thinner: 1 part paint should be mixed with as much as 8 parts water.

Colourwashing

Colourwashing imitates the appearance of old-fashioned, distemper-painted walls and, as such, is particularly appropriate today, when natural, texture-rich interiors are popular. Some specialist paint suppliers continue to stock distemper, but it is relatively simple to recreate the same rough, slightly chalky look with thinned emulsion.

Because of the essentially uneven appearance of a colourwashed finish, it is a simple technique to master and looks particularly good on walls with a slightly irregular surface.

Before embarking on painting a whole wall with a special technique, try out your chosen effect, either on a piece of board or on an inconspicuous corner of the wall. This will give you a chance to perfect the finish you require, and an opportunity to see how the colours work together. Cover your practice area with a coat of paint, allow to dry and start work on the rest of the wall.

Glazes and washes

Glazes

Transparent, oil-based glaze can be bought ready-made, but you can tint proprietary oil glaze to match a colour exactly. To make a basic tinted glaze, mix 1 part glaze with 3–4 parts white spirit and 25ml (1tbsp) white eggshell per 500ml (approx. 1pt) of glaze, using universal stainers to add colour.

A glaze must be applied over non-porous paint, such as eggshell. Depending on the composition, it may take up to two days to dry hard, which gives you plenty of time to correct and rework if you get it wrong first time. For this reason, glaze is easier to handle as an amateur than a wash (see below).

If you are preparing your own glaze rather than using a ready-made one, it is essential to mix up enough for the whole project before you start, because it is almost impossible to duplicate a colour exactly later.

Because this is a very wet wash, ensure that you have covered everything that is not to be painted before you start.

Apply a coat of emulsion to the wall and allow it to dry thoroughly. Create the colour-wash by thinning emulsion paint: 1 part paint to 4–8 parts water and then experiment on a small area until you find a mixture that is both easy to work with and which creates the soft gradations of colour you require. Using a large decorating brush, apply the wash in random, bold, criss-cross strokes over

an area of approx. 1sq m (1sq yd); do not attempt to cover the whole wall. Then, take a slightly damp paintbrush and go over the wash to soften the brushmarks and wipe up any drips.

Do not worry if the walls look very messy and unattractive at this stage. Leave this coat to dry overnight, or for at least 12 hours, and it will improve with the wait.

Repeat the wash technique, again working on 1sq m (1sq yd) at a time. This time apply criss-cross strokes to the areas you

missed the first time. If you are working in a heavy-use or humid area such as a hallway or bathroom, it is possible that the finished effect would benefit from a protective coat of matt polyurethane varnish.

Dry brushing

Dry brushing creates a rougher, more intensely dramatic effect than both glazing and colourwashing. First of all you need to apply a base coat of matt emulsion, and then pour some emulsion in your chosen top-coat colour into a paint tray.

Dip a wide, hard-bristled decorating brush into the paint and scrape off the excess against the tray's ridges or on a wooden board. Then, with cross-hatching strokes (as with colourwashing), apply the top coat. It is very important for this effect – as the name suggests – that you make sure that you keep the brush very dry and that you apply the paint in light strokes using the tip of the brush rather than its flat surface. Allow some of the base colour to show through to evoke a slightly misty effect.

For a greater depth of colour and more intensity, repeat the process, having first allowed the paint to dry thoroughly overnight, or for at least 12 hours anyway. And once again, you may wish to finish the effect with a coat of matt varnish.   ▷

▲ *Although a simple technique to master, two-colour colourwashing in the right colour combination can bring grandeur to a plain wall. Here, the layers of wash have been built up deliberately in some areas more than others, so that the varying degree to which the base colour shows through creates a sense of texture.*

▶ *Dry brushing is a great technique to use with strong colours, the dramatic texture of the cross-hatched brushstrokes enhancing vibrant shades; here green and yellow zing off each other. Equally, if you find solid colour boring, dry brushing a lighter emulsion over a darker tone can create a slightly distressed look.*

Dragging

If you are looking for an elegant, softly striped effect which can enhance doors and wood panelling as well as walls, dragging is the technique you need to master. The background colour shows through the top coat as a series of fine, uneven stripes of colour.

Dragging requires a steady hand and is more tricky than washing or glazing, because of keeping the brushstrokes even along a run of wall. For beginners, it might be a good idea to start on a small area such as the panels of a door. If you are going to use this effect on walls, it is imperative that the surface is smooth and free of bumps (see pages 12–13).

Either an oil-based glaze or a diluted emulsion top coat can be used for dragging, although the oil-based version looks considerably more grand. Remember that emulsion dries faster than oil-based paint, so it may be

easier for a beginner to start with an oil-based glaze: it will give you more time to work on the finish and even allows you to wipe the whole thing off and start again.

Apply two coats of eggshell paint to the wall and leave them to dry thoroughly. Next, apply a coat of oil-based glaze, working from top to bottom, and painting an area that is small enough to work on easily: a vertical strip 60cm (2ft) wide is usually practical.

Before the glaze or paint begins to dry, quickly drag a long-haired, dry flogger from the top of the wall to the bottom in a long, even stroke. It is important to move on to the next area before the edge dries. Clean excess glaze from the brush with a lint-free rag before starting each stroke.

If you use emulsion, use a mid-sheen paint as a base and be careful not to add too much water to the wash at once. Once the oil or

water-based glaze has dried, protect the finish with a coat of matt varnish – or, for an even better result, several coats.

Rag rolling

A quick and easy technique suitable for a beginner, rag rolling is also an excellent way of disguising less-than-perfect walls. The more virulent colour combinations of the 1980s have been replaced by more stylish combinations where the colour of the base coat is similar to that of the top coat: try pale pastels over creamy white for a smart effect.

Oil-based paint is more suitable for rag rolling than water-based paint because of the quick drying time of the latter. However, you can use a mid-sheen emulsion if you so wish; the technique is the same.

Paint the surface with two coats of eggshell or mid-sheen emulsion and leave to dry. Prepare the tinted oil- or water-based glaze and dip a lint-free rag or chamois leather into the mixture, ensuring that the cloth is evenly soaked to avoid blotches on the wall. Squeeze out and roll it up into a loose sausage. Roll the cloth gently over the wall's surface in a random motion.

For a gentler effect, try rag rolling off. Having painted the dried base coat with a top coat of oil- or water-based glaze, roll a clean rag across the glaze to expose the colour beneath. For an even softer look, go over the surface with a softening brush about half an hour after rolling off.

Sponging on

One of the speediest techniques, sponging on is one of the easiest to master. Again, it looks better if the two colours you choose are similar in tone and intensity. You can achieve a richer look by sponging two different shades over the base coat.

Apply two even coats of eggshell or emulsion. Mix the glaze or wash and pour it into a paint tray. Soak a natural sponge in water for the emulsion wash, or in white spirit for an oil-based glaze; wring it out carefully.

Dip the sponge into the paint and rub off any excess against the ridges of the paint tray. Gently dab the sponge on the wall; wring it out frequently to prevent the paint building

▶ *Rag rolling is not a difficult technique to get right. The mottled finish it produces works particularly well with a bold colour choice. Here, a wonderful shade of sky blue swirling over a white base makes the most of the natural daylight, and the total effect perfectly suits the rough texture of the wooden piece in front.*

Paint effects

1 For colourwashing, apply the paint in bold, criss-cross strokes across an area of approximately 1sq m (1sq yd).

2 For a smart effect, drag a long-haired, dry flogger from the top of the wall to the bottom in a long, even stroke.

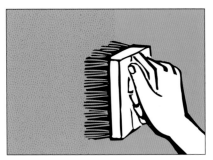

3 Randomly roll a chamois or lint-free cloth soaked in your second shade of paint over the wall's surface.

4 Gently dab a sponge coated in your second colour over the wall. Wring out frequently to prevent ugly splodges.

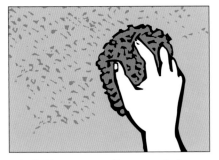

5 Load a large brush with paint and knock the metal part against a ruler. Stand back to check for bare patches.

6 Load stippling brush with paint and remove excess with newspaper. Work slowly down the wall.

up into clumps. If you are using a second colour, wait until the first coat is thoroughly dry before applying it.

Sponging off

Sponging off – like rag rolling off – creates a slightly more subtle, cloudy effect than its technical counterpart.

Brush a coat of tinted oil glaze with the consistency of thick cream over the dried base coat using a wide decorating brush. Working on 1sq m (1sq yd) at a time to avoid the glaze drying out, wring out a sponge in white spirit and dab it swiftly on the wet glaze, lifting some away from the surface.

Bagging is adapted from these techniques. Using a small cloth in a scrunched-up plastic bag, dab the wall in the same way as you did with the sponge to create lively patterns. To prevent blotches of colour, wipe excess paint from the bag from time to time.

Ideally, sponged and bagged walls which could be easily damaged should be sealed with a protective coat of matt varnish.

Spattering

A dramatic and relatively simple process to master, spattering is messy, so before you begin, ensure that the floor is covered with plastic and that you are wearing a mask and eye protection. The effect is cumulative, built up by spattering tiny dots of one or more colours against a base coat; two or even three spattering colours will add to the depth and richness of the effect.

Using a piece of newspaper as your practice wall, load a large decorating brush with paint or glaze and knock the metal part of it against a stick to flick off excess paint until you achieve the size of dots you want. Then, hold the brush parallel to the wall and knock it in the same way against a stick or piece of baton. Continue until the wall is covered in a fine spray of dots; stand back to check for any slightly bare patches and go over it again until the coating is even.

If you are using a second colour, allow the first dots to dry, before repeating the process with a second colour.

Stippling

This effect is best suited to walls in reasonable condition and needs a base of oil-based, non-porous paint in order for it to 'take' evenly. Glazing liquid, eggshell thinned with white spirit or mid-sheen emulsion thinned with water can all be used.

Coat the base colour with a thin film of glaze using a wide decorator's brush, working on 1sq m (1sq yd) at a time. Using a specialist stippling brush, jab the bristles against the wall in sharp, rhythmic strokes, creating an elegantly mottled surface. (Purpose-made stippling brushes can be prohibitively expensive. Although you will not get the same super-sophisticated effect as with a professional brush, it is worth experimenting with any large, firm-bristled brush – a new household broom can be quite a good substitute.) Work swiftly across the area, blending sections together; take care to avoid sliding the brush across the surface as this will create smears. Wipe the stippling bush periodically with a lint-free cloth to remove excess glaze.

Faux finishes

▲ *Walls that imitate materials such as terracotta or plaster are a wonderful foil for relaxed interiors. They look particularly good as a backdrop for wood or sumptuous textiles. Picking out the colour and, as here, the texture of the wall in the furnishings of a room brings cohesion to a scheme that may in fact contain many disparate elements.*

the kind of effect you want to recreate and practise on a piece of paper or board before you embark on your panelling or walls.

Use a soft cloth to rub some transparent oil glaze onto a base of two coats of eggshell. Dip a fine artist's brush into a glaze of the required colour; quickly and gently flick some veins across the paint surface. Do not worry about a few breaks and blobs in the paint; this will add to the finished effect. Using the tip of a softening brush, softly stroke the veins to blur them. Dip a fine artist's brush into white spirit and gently go over the glazed surface, roughly following the lines of some of the veins. Soften the surface again, this time in one direction only. And finally, take a clean softener brush and go lightly over the surface to eliminate any brush marks and create the desired cloudy finish.

Faux bois
Elaborate wood-graining effects that are designed to imitate rich and desirable marks and patterns – those found in burr walnut,

Once you have mastered some basic paint techniques, you may wish to try something a little more adventurous. *Faux* finishes allow you to imitate the effect of wood, stone, fabric and other unusual materials at a fraction of the cost. The key to success is to use a light touch – and to know when to stop. Never be tempted to splash on too much paint; rather, build up the effect in layers.

Draw inspiration from a wide variety of sources. Begin by looking at the real thing – marble, wood grain and stone – then at postcards, books, paintings, even films.

Antiquing
Few people are fortunate enough to live with genuine, original old plaster walls. 'Ageing' a surface is a relatively simple process,

however, and fun to do too. Dry brushing (see pages 18–19) is an effective way of re-creating the effect of an old wall, or you may wish to use layers of paint in slightly different tones. Start with the brightest shade and gradually 'age' the surface with layers of wash, working with the original shade and darkening it by degrees with a little raw umber. Smear on the paint roughly with a brush or cloth and when it is dry, rub gently at the paint surface with some sandpaper or wire wool, revealing glimpses of the original colour and even touches of plaster.

Marbling
There are many different kinds of marble and, consequently, many different kinds of marbling. Study the real thing to decide on

for instance – will take some time to perfect, but even a decorating novice can achieve good basic graining effects.

Choose a suitable base colour – deep red is a good base for a mahogany effect while a pale golden cream creates realistic oak grain – and apply two coats of eggshell. Mix up the graining colour by thinning some transparent oil glaze with white spirit and colouring it with a little artist's oil paint: a dark purplish brown or even black creates a realistic glaze for mahogany, while a little burnt umber can replicate oak. Apply the glaze in an even, dense coat on top of the eggshell.

Take a dusting brush and drag it along the length of the surface in a light sweep. Repeat this sweeping brush-stroke to blur any hard lines. With a clean softener or dusting brush, quickly and gently work across the grain.

Imitation terracotta

Warm 'terracotta' walls are the perfect backdrop for today's ethnically inspired interiors, and a convincing effect is simple to achieve.

Paint the wall with a base coat of matt emulsion in a creamy gold colour. Dilute terracotta-coloured emulsion – equal parts of paint to water – and coat the wall with a wide decorating brush, brushing backwards and forwards over the painted surface, continuing even when the wash begins to dry.

Allow the paint to dry out completely and then take a clean decorating brush dipped in water to dampen down the surface, working on the usual 1sq m (1sq yd) at a time. Dilute some cream-coloured emulsion: mix 1 part paint to 2 parts water. Using a 2.5cm (1in) decorating brush, make a rough pattern of lines across the damp piece of wall. Using a

▲ *The key to successful marbling is subtlety. Here soft creams and greys applied with a very light touch look as appropriate with the wooden floor as they do with the more contemporary chrome table.*

◄ *There are really no limits to the kind of effects you can achieve on your walls. These walls have been given the soft, coppery bloom of verdigris. As with all faux techniques, it is essential that you study the real thing before you start, to ensure that you get the detail right.*

slightly dampened natural sponge, dab at the paint surface to blur and smudge the lines. Keep gently sponging the area until you have achieved the soft, cloudy bloom of terracotta. Use this technique with different colours to imitate lead or unfinished plaster.

Verdigris

To recreate on walls the wonderful blue-green patina of weathered copper, brass or bronze, start with a dark brown coat of matt emulsion. When it has dried, stipple a light covering of bright turquoise green over the entire surface, allowing a trace of the base colour to show through. Repeat the process in some areas, making the turquoise deeper.

Then look at a real piece of verdigris to get an exact colour match for the kind of effect you want and choose a bright shade of green. Go over parts of the turquoise green with a stipple brush. And finally, with a very light hand and an almost dry brush, stipple some of the wall once more – with faint traces of dark gold or bronze paint.

Finally apply a coat of matt varnish; you might perhaps like to mix a little white paint into it to dull the finish slightly.

Faux leather

A leather effect in deep oxblood, bottle green or dark brown can look very smart, particularly when used to add richness to a small space. Using a small to medium-sized decorating brush, stipple the wall thickly with a paler-coloured matt emulsion than the finished effect you are looking for. Allow to dry for at least 24 hours.

Repeat the process with a darker shade of emulsion, this time splaying and twisting the brush as you work to create texture. Allow this layer to dry, again for at least 24 hours.

Mix some artist's oil paint – one part raw umber to one part burnt sienna – into a transparent oil glaze and rub this over the surface of the wall with a cloth; take another soft cloth and gently but thoroughly rub off the excess glaze, allowing the texture of the emulsion to show through. In places, rub the surface with fine sandpaper to reveal some of the emulsion, but ultimately protect the surface with a semi-matt varnish.

Trompe l'oeil

Paint is a truly versatile material which, provided you have time and patience on your side, allows you to create a huge range of decorative effects for relatively little cost.

Trompe l'oeil painting has a lineage almost as long as the history of painting. Although it tends to bring to mind the grandiose ceilings of Italian palazzi or mural schemes in the great country houses, this is nothing more than a great misconception. The term means 'an accomplished visual trick' – and whether you want to reproduce a vista on a wall, or a grisaille frieze, or an eighteenth-century 'book door', or the effect of tiles or marble, sandstone or granite, *trompe l'oeil* is the name of the game. It is merely a question of playing a witty visual trick on the passer-by.

Painting a mural

Whilst not necessarily possessing the creative or technical abilities of Mantegna, Tiepolo or Veronese, you should not be frightened of trying to create a grand pictorial effect for yourself in your own home. You could add a sumptuous garden view to a windowless room, or create a fantastic landscape mural on an entire wall, or you could complement a simple period scheme with painted architectural detailing: just consider which seems most appropriate to the scale and function of the room. What is more, *trompe l'oeil* painting is ideal for having fun; exaggeration and weird perspective may result in a surreal effect, but that may be just what you want – a visual diversion and a talking point!

Perhaps you have been inspired by an illustration in a book or magazine; in a way this would be an easier course to pursue than working from scratch if your artistic skills are limited because all the basic techniques of copying an image from a book are relatively easy to master. Someone else has done the difficult bit, making all the elements of the image work together; all you need to do is scale up the image to fit the chosen site.

The first thing to do is to trace the design onto tracing paper using pen or pencil and then draw a grid over it, numbering each square. Next, draw a grid directly onto the wall, with the same number of squares, numbered to correspond with your original grid.

▲ *Successful* trompe l'oeil *painting requires a substantial level of skill, but the finished result is worth the work. You can expand a small space or contract a large one, and even create an Aegean seascape in the middle of a city, with views of islands across the bay – the stuff of daydreams, the perfect setting for a cosy armchair and a good book.*

Squaring up

1 Copy the desired image onto tracing paper, simplifying it for clarity, and then draw a grid of squares over it.

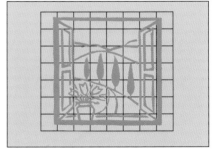

2 Draw another grid on the wall, and sketch in the main lines of the design as a painting guide, square by square.

Fake tiles

1 Create a wall of 'tiles' with a small roller. Work in horizontal rows; uneven edges add to the handmade effect.

2 Vertical bands of diamond-shaped tiles are equally quick and simple; use a small roller held diagonally.

It is worth remembering to prepare your wall with a base coat of paint before you transfer your design. Then copy the traced design closely onto the wall in pen or soft pencil, using the grid to guide you. Work square by square; it may help to look at each square as a series of abstract lines, rather than as part of the whole scheme; you can always soften up the junctions between the squares once you have copied all of them. It may help also to fix the traced design onto the wall using masking tape as a constant reference; you should always stand back and take stock as you work. Do not pay too much attention to detail at this stage as you only want a sketched guide. If you define everything too rigidly, you will find it very difficult to paint freely and this will most likely result in a stiff, lifeless design. Once your sketch exists, start painting and be bold!

If you are not confident about your technique with a paintbrush, do not struggle with an ambitious project in the vain hope of producing a masterpiece. Try decoupage to recreate decorative plasterwork rather than trying to reproduce a Renaissance frieze freehand. If you have access to a photocopier and your desired motif is reasonably small-scale, it is obviously very easy to enlarge or shrink a design mechanically, and to repeat a motif for a border. Or mock up panels using stone-effect paper, antiquing it with a tinted glaze.

In a kitchen or bathroom, it might be more appropriate to think simple, and to use a small radiator roller to create a quick and effective tile effect. Load the roller evenly and paint rows of tiles – either horizontally or as diamonds – leaving a 'grout' space between each 'tile' for a more realistic look.

◄ *Trompe l'oeil can be as elaborate as the sea view (left) or as simple as a couple of runs of tiles, here. It is important that you match your aspirations to your level of skill, but almost anyone could have a stab at this effect.*

Stripes, checks and patterns

▲ *Paint allows you to get the effect of hand-blocked wallpaper at a fraction of the cost. This sophisticated looking lattice was created by painting a red top coat over the undercoat which had been covered in criss-crossed masking tape.*

Making stripes

Stripes and checks comprise a decorating trend that never goes out of fashion; they have a striking, graphic quality, and a fresh, well-ordered, clean-cut appearance, whether or not their edges are sharp, making them suitable for practically any situation – in combination with areas of plain colour or with each other. Hugely versatile, stripes and checks are equally varied in their effect; wide stripes will be bolder than narrower ones, or you can create a more sophisticated rhythm, following one wide with three narrow stripes, for instance, and then repeating it.

Think too about the effect of colour on your chosen stripes; you could create a stunningly dramatic study using dark paint and wide stripes, provided that you could then light it efficiently, but that combination would not work in a kitchen or dining room, where a fresher and lighter effect would be better. All you need is a little patience, a plumb line, your paint and tools.

The quickest, simplest method of creating stripes is to paint the wall in your chosen base colour and then use a roller to create stripes in a contrasting shade using a plumb line to guide you. If you wish to create broader stripes than it is possible to paint with a roller, mark out the area to be painted with masking tape before you start, again using a plumb line to establish a true vertical. If you like stripes but are wary of the crisp, bandbox look, roughly and lightly paint in your stripes and then immediately go over the wet paint with a dry roller to create a

Making stripes

1 Use a plumb line to mark out vertical stripes. Use a soft pencil and a very light touch.

2 With the pencil marks to guide you, carefully paint the stripes with a wide roller.

slightly distressed effect. A smaller, 'pin-stripe' effect can be created by cutting a foam roller into narrow stripes, using tape to keep each part of the roller separate.

You could use this stripe both vertically and horizontally, and in more than one colour, to create a chequered effect.

Using patterned rollers

Patterned rollers have been used to decorate walls for several centuries. They are enjoying a popular revival today because they are easy to use and create interesting effects cheaply – either with colour or with textured paint. You can make your own, or specialist suppliers stock rollers and rockers for more difficult effects – from wood graining to damask.

Using textured paint

Apart from the practical aspects of textured paint, and it is very useful for covering less than perfect surfaces, its aesthetic potential is much under-rated. You can buy a range of patterned roller sleeves specifically for textured paint and with a little time, effort and imagination, it is possible to achieve sophisticated, sculpted effects for relatively little.

▶ *Few paint effects are simpler to achieve or more dramatic in appearance than stripes. In this country-style bedroom, all four walls have been painted with wide stripes. Marked out using masking tape and a plumb line and then roughly painted in deep red, they are bold and yet far from brash, producing an all-American look.*

3 If you are worried about creating precise edges, use masking tape to mark off the lines.

4 To create narrow stripes, divide the roller in two with an elastic band.

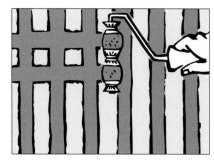

5 To create checks, use the roller to go across the vertical lines in a horizontal band.

Stamping, stencilling and gilding

▶ *Stamping is the ideal paint technique if you're short of time – or skill. A repeat design, such as this simple pattern of hearts stamped onto a colourwashed wall, gives a dramatic effect, but takes only a matter of hours to carry out.*

design onto an acetate sheet and cut out with a sharp knife. Attach to the wall with masking tape or spray adhesive.

Next, apply the colour. Whether you are using a stencil brush or a spray can, the secret is a light touch. With a spray can, waft it quickly and gently over the surface, gradually building up the colour in subtle layers. If using a stencil brush, rub it on a piece of paper towel until almost all the paint has been removed from the head of the brush, then stipple or swirl it over the stencil. Remove the stencil, reposition and repeat the process.

Gilding

Few decorating projects are more satisfying than working with gold leaf. However, the expense of the material puts it far outside the pocket of most amateur decorators. There is no reason, though, why you should deprive yourself of using lustrous metallic materials in small quantities, perhaps on a motif against

Stamping

Compared to other paint effects, stamping really can be, quite literally, child's play. Make your own stamps from medium to high-density foam in the same way as a child makes potato-cut stamps, drawing on a design and then cutting away the excess foam with a scalpel. Stick the sponge onto a piece of wood and attach a small door knob to the back of it to make application easier. If, however, you would rather buy a stamp, there are many outlets that now stock a wide range of designs made from rubber or foam, thus making them very hard-wearing.

Apply the paint either with a roller or by dipping the stamp into a plate containing a small amount of paint. Ensure an even coating and then set to work, taking your design across the whole wall.

Stencilling

This is one of the cheapest ways to provide a decorative finish. Use stencils to create a dramatic pictorial effect or use a motif to create a border or all-over pattern at a fraction of the cost of wallpaper. Choose from the enormous selection of pre-cut stencils available or make your own. Draw your

Stamping

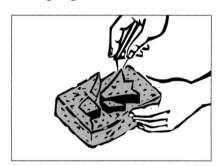

1 First draw the outline of your design onto the sponge. Cut away the surrounding areas using a scalpel.

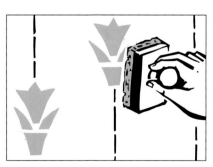

2 For large-scale patterns, chalk guidelines onto the wall. Coat the sponge evenly with paint and dab on firmly.

Stencilling

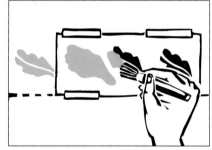

1 Remove excess paint from the brush with a paper towel before swirling or stippling it lightly over the stencil.

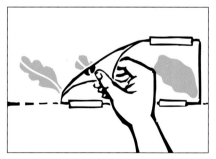

2 Gently peel off the stencil, taking care not to smudge the paint, and reposition it.

a wall painted in a deep rich colour such as lacquer red, midnight blue or forest green. Dutch metal leaf or aluminium leaf are less expensive alternatives to the real thing. Aluminium leaf can be made to gleam like gold with one or two coats of orange shellac. These, and the substances mentioned below, are available from specialist decorating outlets.

First, give the wall to be gilded a coat of flat or mid-sheen oil-based paint. Decide on your design or motif and either draw it free-hand on the wall or use a stencil as a guide. Paint the areas to be gilded with ready-made red gesso for Dutch metal, or cobalt blue casein for silver or aluminium leaf. When this is dry, paint on a thin layer of goldsize, following the manufacturer's instructions. When the goldsize is only slightly tacky, gently press on a sheet of leaf, leaf-side down, on the sized area. Carefully peel away the leaf's wax backing and lay down the next sheet so that it slightly overlaps with the first. Continue until you have built up your pattern. Leave for several hours to dry and rub off the loose leaf with a soft cloth; the rest of the leaf should remain in the sized area of your motif.

Finish off by varnishing the whole surface with a clear, semi-gloss oil-based varnish.

For those who long for glitter, it is also worth checking out the wide range of metallic paints, powders, creams and pens on the market. These can be put to a wide range of decorating uses, from painting a whole wall to picking out moulding detail.

Gilding

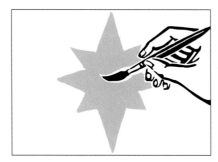

1 Paint the motif in red gesso or cobalt blue casein. When dry, paint a layer of goldsize over the top.

2 When the goldsize is only slightly tacky, press on the sheet, leaf-side down.

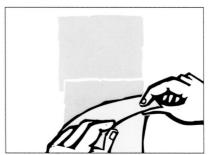

3 Carefully peel away the wax backing and apply the next sheet, overlapping the first slightly. Let dry overnight.

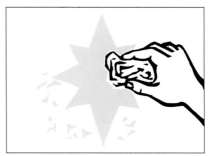

4 Rub off the excess leaf with a soft cloth, leaving the original motif intact.

▲ *Given the costs involved, it makes sense to restrict the use of gilding to small areas. This random design of horizontal and vertical gold blocks is restrained but nonetheless extremely effective, giving interest to plain white walls and mirroring the angular patterns of the parquet flooring.*

Problems with paintwork

Most flaws in paint surfaces can be avoided if you are scrupulous in your preparation and always use the correct materials. Even with the utmost care, however, some problems may occur, but these can usually be salvaged and sometimes do not entail too much extra work.

Blistering

This is caused by moisture or air trapped beneath a coat of oil-based paint. The answer is to strip off the paint, carefully fill any holes and then repaint. With wood, it may be necessary to prime, undercoat and then repaint.

Flaking

When the new surface reacts badly to what is underneath it, flaking occurs. Emulsion paint, for example, can flake when painted over a high-gloss finish or distemper. Unfortunately if this occurs there is no alternative but to strip the flaking surface, get back to the base, prepare it again properly and paint the area again.

Wrinkling

If you apply a second coat of oil-based paint, such as eggshell, before the first coat has dried thoroughly, the surface may wrinkle. Strip the paint and reapply it.

Runs and drips

Possibly the most common problem, runs and drips are caused by loading too much paint onto the brush. Let the paint dry, rub the proud blobs gently with fine-grade sandpaper, remove the dust created by the sandpaper and touch up with fresh paint.

Paint faults

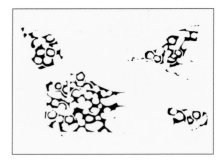

1 Blistering is caused by air trapped beneath a coat of paint. It has to be stripped off and the surface repainted.

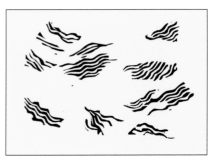

2 The only solution to an area that is flaking is to strip the area back to the original surface and begin again.

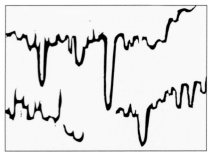

3 Drips can be corrected by rubbing them flat with sandpaper, cleaning off the dust and repainting.

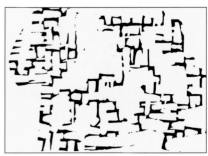

4 Crazing occurs when the top coat of paint reacts badly with the surface beneath. Strip off and repaint.

▲ *Strong blocks of contrasting solid colour can work wonderfully if walls are in good condition and prepared thoroughly. When using strong colours, however, it is wise to create some kind of continuity. Here, the midnight blue dining room has a terracotta picture rail and yellow stained chairs to continue the scheme from the living room.*

◀ *Cloudy colourwashing, rubbed on with a cloth rather than applied with a brush, is a wonderfully speedy technique perfectly suited to the style of this country interior. Paint treatments that have the effect, visually, of texturizing the surface are suited to walls that may have minor imperfections such as slightly uneven plastering.*

Cleaning equipment

1 Clean off excess paint under running cold water. Then wash in a weak solution of warm water and detergent.

2 Prolong the life of a roller by rinsing out emulsion paint under a cold running tap until the water turns clear.

Crazing

This occurs when a layer of new paint reacts badly with a painted surface underneath, or if layers of paint have different drying times. The only option is to repaint, removing all the layers of paint and preparing the surface again from scratch.

Grit, dust or insects in the paint

If this occurs, wait until the paint dries, then sand the area gently with fine sandpaper and wipe off the dust. If you sand lightly enough, you may not need to touch up the paint.

Stains in paintwork

Stains occur when insufficient preparation is done before the emulsion is applied. Mineral salts, moulds and other residues and impurities can react badly with the water in emulsion and will seep through the surface. Get back to the original surface and coat it with a proprietary primer-sealer and when that has dried, repaint.

Poor coverage

This is most likely to show when you are applying a light colour over a dark base. Streaky flashes of the base colour will appear under the top coat. Apply further coats of paint, until you have a solid top colour.

Cleaning equipment

Cleaning your equipment after you have finished painting will significantly prolong its life. Brushes, rollers and pads that have been used with emulsion or other water-based paints should be rinsed with cold water to remove excess paint, paying particular attention to the base of the bristles, and then washed in a weak solution of warm water and detergent to remove the residue.

Equipment used for oil-based paint or varnish should be cleaned with turpentine, white spirit or a proprietary cleaner, ensuring that it is worked well into the bristles or pile. When all the paint has been removed, all equipment should be rinsed thoroughly in warm water and shaken vigorously to remove the excess.

To keep their shape, brushes can be wrapped in clean paper towels fixed with masking tape. Hang up brushes and rollers, and place pads face-up to maintain the pile, and your equipment should last you for years.

Paper and fabric

Many home decorators are hesitant about
hanging wallpaper themselves because they
imagine that it will be terribly difficult to
achieve a professional finish. However, if
the task is approached in a methodical way
and the chosen paper is not too difficult to
handle and match, you may be surprised
how easy and satisfying it is to put up
your own paper.

After many years in the decorative wilderness, wallpapers seem to be enjoying something of a revival. The enormous selection of designs available, and the ability of paper to disguise everything from cracked walls to clumsy proportions, make them a great resource for the decorator.

Whether you want to recreate the look of a Palladian villa, a Victorian boudoir or a 1950s diner, you will find that there are papers on the market to make your task easier. And once you have chosen your main paper, you can turn your attention to the many co-ordinating borders and friezes that will create a more 'finished' job. They can be used in combination with wallpaper, by themselves to pep up painted walls, or to create architectural interest where it is lacking. Indeed, such combinations seem to tap into the mood of the moment, for they tend to allow the feeling of an easy layering of pattern and texture to predominate.

Basic principles

Having decided to be brave and work with wallpaper, there are several basic principles to follow to get maximum mileage from the wallpaper you choose.

Wallpaper is a great ally when you want to play optical tricks with a space. Use it to expand or contract the space in which you are working, or to draw the eye away from ugly but immovable features. Turning to the detail of the matter, dark colours and heavy patterns will generally make a room seem smaller, while pale, loosely patterned ones – and large trellised papers too – will make the room seem larger, and vertical stripes on the walls tend to make low ceilings appear higher.

In general, rooms that are used a lot prefer plainer papers because heavy patterns can be wearing on the eye, and are therefore tiring to live with. They are also more difficult to mix with other furnishings, particularly if you do not have the well-experienced decorator's touch.

One of the aspects governing the revival of interest in wallpaper is technology. Wallpapers are now easier to hang than ever before, not least because of the ready-pasted varieties, and can be used with ease on a far greater variety of surfaces than they used to be. So, while in the past wallpapering was seen as a daunting prospect for almost all but the most experienced of decorators, nowadays that dubious reputation is beginning to be dispelled as myth. And justifiably

▲ *Walls don't have to be covered with wallpaper – there are many different techniques that could be used to achieve an interesting effect. Here, the walls have been covered in brown packaging paper to provide a cheap but smart covering. Other sorts of paper can also be used. Try sticking up sheets of music, photocopies of old prints or even pictures cut out from magazines.*

◄ *Wallpaper can be used in any part of the house, even the bathroom. Papers are available in different weights and for different uses. Here, a vinyl-coated wallpaper has been used to combat potential problems from heat, damp and humidity.*

so, for with the correct equipment and a methodical approach, wallpapering is a relatively straightforward task to get right – on most of the walls in a home.

At its most basic, wallpapering with plain lining paper is a way of covering less-than-perfect walls in preparation for painting or papering with a decorative paper. Even a beginner can tackle this, as it does not require the matching of difficult patterns and repeats.

Lining paper can be purchased in several thicknesses, and it is definitely easier to work with the heavier ones because they are less likely to stretch or tear as you work. If you are daunted by the prospect of papering but it is really the only option for the room you are decorating, give yourself some confidence by tackling a small job like lining a room and then move on to a more ambitious project with a patterned paper.

If your skills have not been tested, or you consider yourself unskilled, there are several basic guidelines you can follow to make your life easier: buy ready-pasted wallpaper; be cautious about using strong patterns as they are harder to measure up for and more difficult to hang; and avoid cheaper papers as they have a tendency to tear. (It is a false economy to think that you should buy cheaper paper in order not to waste money if everything goes wrong, because the reality is that it is far more likely to go wrong if you do. Be bold and buy good-quality paper in the first place and you are more likely both to do a good job and to achieve a good finish.)

Whatever your level of skill, buy all the wallpaper you need for a job in one go in order to avoid variations in colour, and always buy one more roll than you have calculated as being needed just in case your calculations are slightly inaccurate. And the best tip comes from the professionals: always, always clear up as you go along. Although getting rid of damp scraps of paper and wiping up paste smears as they occur may seem enormously time-consuming, it is this kind of attention to detail that can make all the difference between a shoddy job and one that looks enviably professional.

Directory of wallpaper and vinyl

There is a massive range of wallpapers available, in every kind of finish – from traditional patterns to imitation paint effects. Decoratively, the possibilities are endless. Practically, some papers are more suitable for some tasks than others.

Cheap papers tend to be thin and are therefore tricky to handle and consequently more difficult to hang. They are also more liable to show wear and tear. Sturdier – and therefore more expensive – papers are usually a better investment.

Most rolls come in standard sizes: 10m (33ft) long and 52cm (20½in) wide. Fabric papers are generally exorbitantly expensive – so much so that they are sometimes sold like fabric, by the metre.

Most papers are treated to repel moisture to different degrees: spongeable papers can be wiped clean; washable papers can be washed with water. Vinyls, which are coated with a tough plastic, can be scrubbed clean.

Textured papers are very good for covering small cracks and other minor imperfections in the wall surface. Lending a variety to the texture of surfaces in a room is a good alternative to using a variety of colours or tones.

Woodchip

A tough, durable paper designed to cover small imperfections in wall and ceiling surfaces. It is inexpensive and is supplied in an off-white colour, to be painted to match the room's colour scheme. It is extremely difficult to remove once it is in place and has rather fallen out of favour recently. If your walls are imperfect, go for a more interesting relief paper such as anaglypta, or for a distressed paint finish for a more dramatic effect. **1**

Lining

Heavy-duty off-white paper which is applied to walls after any levelling out of the plaster but before any painting

and papering. It is used to achieve a smooth, professional finish, and can be bought in five different thicknesses.

Vinyl

Possibly the most widely available species of wallpaper, vinyl is now obtainable in a massive variety of designs, many with co-ordinating borders or friezes. A paper backing is covered with a layer of waterproof vinyl, thus making the surface extremely durable as it can be sponged down without risk of spoiling the finish. Easy to hang and remove, vinyl is available with an unglued or ready-pasted backing. If you intend to use an unpasted paper, it is advisable to use a fungicidal adhesive to prevent mould from growing underneath.

Embossed

Available in a wide selection of relief patterns, from floral designs to patterns imitating wood panelling, ready to be finished with gloss or emulsion paint. Their hard-wearing finish makes them popular for the area below the dado in hallways and for any walls with a less-than-perfect finish; once painted, their tough surface is washable.

Lincrusta has a texture that can resemble anything from tiles to wood grain. A solid paper backing is coated with a pliable filler and linseed oil. This is pressed into a pattern while soft, and once hard gives a tough, scrubbable wall-covering, particularly when coated with eggshell or a high-gloss oil-based paint, as many manufacturers recommend, especially if it is being used in a heavy traffic area.

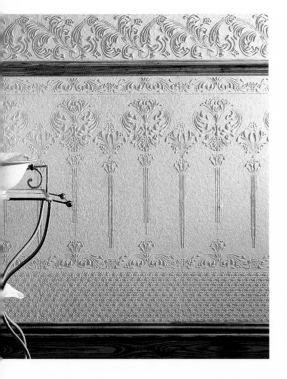

Anaglypta is a lighter, more flexible paper than lincrusta, but its finish is also extremely durable. It is made from two layers of paper, pressed together and embossed with a huge variety of relief patterns.   **2**

Hand-block-printed

These papers come in a huge variety of designs and their quality and depth of colour cannot be surpassed. They are, however, expensive to buy. To defray the costs and make a little paper go a long way you could consider hanging them as panels edged by narrow wooden moulding, or using them above or below the dado in combination with a less expensive paper or paint. They are bought unpasted and hanging them requires great diligence.   **4**

Machine-printed

The most widely available kind of wallpaper, machine-printed papers come in a huge variety of designs and finishes and are less expensive than

hand-blocked paper. They can sometimes be dressed up with a coat of matt polyurethane varnish.   **5**

Foamed polyethylene

A soft, lightweight paper, also called Novamura. Comes in a wide range of designs and is relatively easy to hang.

Friezes and borders

Wallpaper ranges now nearly always include a series of co-ordinating borders or friezes, which means that making a decision about detailing and finishing can be completely straightforward. However, you should feel free to create different effects, using more original combinations, and picking up on painted finishes too. Borders and friezes are sold in rolls and are roughly 7.5–30cm (3–12in) wide. And although friezes are usually hung horizontally at the level of the skirting board, dado rail or picture rail, borders can also be used to create 'panels', by making up squares or rectangles.   **3**

Preparing the surface for wallpapering

▶ *Wallpapers come in a dazzling selection of finishes and styles, from rustic to romantic, from delicate hand-blocked to tough vinyl. This country-style paper is strikingly pretty but has a washable surface – invaluable in a kitchen.*

As with painting, the quality of the finish you will achieve with wallpaper is dependent upon thorough preparation. A new wallpaper will transform the look of a room but it will not necessarily hide the basic defects of the wall beneath. Some textured papers, such as woodchip or anaglypta, will successfully cover minor imperfections, but smooth-finish papers can be extremely unforgiving.

Prepare for wallpapering in the same way as you would for painting (see pages 12–13) by moving as much furniture as you can out of the room and pushing the rest into the centre where you can cover it with dust sheets. You will need to cover the floor in plastic sheeting which should then be covered by a fabric dust sheet, to prevent you slipping on the wet plastic. Stripping old wallpaper is an extremely damp process, so it is also vital that you pay attention to your own safety while you do it. Because of the amount of water you are using, you may wish to turn off the power temporarily at the mains while you strip the paper near light switches, electrical sockets and other fittings.

Preparation

It is very important to remove old wallpaper properly and then rectify any damage to the wall beneath before starting to paper. Left untreated, damp patches will eventually seep through, and impurities in the plaster could eventually spoil the paper. It is essential to investigate any problems at this stage and have them dealt with before wasting money on decorating what may then have to be redone.

Stripping old wallpaper

Vinyl papers are generally the simplest to remove. In fact, many of them are specifically designed so that you can simply peel them off the wall. Gently pull at the patterned top layer and it should begin to separate from the plain backing, leaving a layer of what amounts to lining paper on which to hang the new design. Sometimes, however, this paper is too damaged to use effectively as lining paper and if this is so, you will have to soak and scrape the paper to reach the smoother layer beneath.

Non-peelable vinyls and other papers need to be dampened to loosen the adhesive before you can remove them. There are several methods of getting the moisture to penetrate the paper's surface. The simplest way is to use the corner of a wallpaper scraper gently to score the paper, taking care not to press so hard as to make indentations on the plaster beneath; alternatively, there are scoring tools which you can simply move across the paper's surface. They leave tiny holes in the paper to allow the water to penetrate effectively without harming the wall.

Next, allow warm, soapy water to soak into the surface. Use a hand-held sprayer or a sponge to apply the solution, working from the top so that the water runs down the wall, presoaking the lower part of the wall. When the water has soaked in properly, you can begin to scrape the wall using a scraper or wallpaper remover, using the sponge to resoak any particularly stubborn areas.

Alternatively, hire or buy a steam stripper, which will almost undoubtedly cut down your preparation time considerably: the heat and moisture of the steam work quickly to loosen the glue.

When you think you have removed all the paper, go over the whole wall again, lightly scraping and wiping away any residue of paper or glue which may still be stuck to the wall. Carefully fill any dents or cracks and deal with any impurities such as mould growth or mineral-salt build-up (see pages 12–13).

Sizing

Size reduces the absorbency of a plaster wall. Thus sizing makes hanging paper easier because the adhesive adheres more readily to the sealed wall. Size should be applied to prepared walls – which have been allowed to dry out completely after soaking or steaming – using a large pasting brush. When you have finished, wipe any drips of size off woodwork using a damp cloth.

Lining paper and cross-lining

If your walls are marred with minor cracks, cover them up with lining paper to provide a smooth surface for paint or decorative paper. Medium-grade paper is normally used on walls; thicker paper is used on ceilings as it is less likely to tear as you put it up. As with decorative paper, follow the manufacturer's directions on the type of size and paste to use and allow the paper plenty of time to dry out, usually overnight, before hanging decorative paper over the top.

If you are going to paint the wall, the lining paper is usually pasted vertically. However, if you were to adopt this method under wallpaper, there is a risk that the seams from the different papers would fall in the same places, and this would cause unsightly ridges. To prevent this, you should cross-line the walls, hanging the lining paper horizontally rather than vertically. The essential method is the same, whichever the orientation: measure the walls, making sure the tape measure is strictly horizontal, and cut the paper into lengths, as you would when hanging a decorative paper vertically. Starting at the top of the wall and working down to the skirting board, hang the paper from side to side.

Stripping old wallpaper

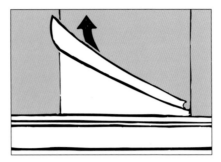

1 Modern vinyl papers are usually designed so that you can simply peel them off the wall.

2 Other papers require dampening. Scoring the surface diagonally with a scraper allows moisture to penetrate.

3 Next, apply warm, soapy water with a sponge or spray. Allow the paper to soak, then peel off with a scraper.

4 Using a steam stripper is a fast, effective way to loosen the glue. The paper can then be removed with a scraper.

Applying lining paper

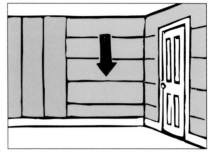

1 If you are using lining paper under wallpaper, the wall should be cross-lined to avoid unsightly ridges.

2 Hang lining paper in horizontal strips; concertina each strip in one hand and unfold it as you go.

Tools and equipment

Preparation

- **Plastic bucket:** for warm, soapy water and to mix size.
- **Sponge:** to soak paper in order to remove it.
- **Hand sprayer:** to soak paper, instead of a sponge.
- **Wallpaper steamer:** a machine that helps to remove paper; ideal when stripping large areas. Expensive, so you may wish to hire it.
- **Scraper:** to score and remove paper.
- **Wallpaper scorer:** a more sophisticated tool for scoring paper.
- **Size:** use the brand recommended by the manufacturer to match the paper of your choice.
- **Wooden dowel:** to mix size.
- **Large decorating/pasting brush:** to apply size.
- **Sponge:** to clean up.
- **Plastic refuse sacks:** in order to facilitate tidying up as you progress with the work.

Planning

Pattern matching

The thought of matching patterns is perhaps one of the most daunting aspects of hanging your own wallpaper. However, so long as you purchase sufficient paper and take some time and trouble with matching it up at the cutting stage, this process is, in fact, relatively straightforward.

A plain paper, or one with a continuous or small, random pattern, such as vertical stripes or a tiny floral print, does not need matching. You can simply cut equal lengths straight from the roll; all you need to remember is to add 10cm (4in) to each length (to allow for 5cm [2in] overlaps at each end).

To match other, more complicated designs, lay the cut strip of paper design-side up on the pasting table, and then lay another strip beside it, matching the pattern as accurately as you can on the adjoining widths, and then ensure that you add the standard 5cm (2in) at each end to the measured matching drop to allow for the overhang – a total of 10cm (4in).

Check, before you cut, that the two drops have the same number of pattern repeats, and that each has an overhang allowance. A straight-match pattern has the same part of the design running symmetrically down each side of the paper. This kind of paper is not very difficult to hang. All you need to remember is, once again, to add enough allowance at each end to line up the pattern exactly; you do not need to match adjoining strips horizontally.

On a drop-match pattern the motifs are staggered, which means that you have to add extra in the cutting: the amount of stagger in the pattern – or length of pattern repeat – is usually indicated on the roll. You could try cutting alternate drops from different rolls, but this may prove more confusing than helpful.

Establishing a vertical

It goes without saying that hanging your first strip of paper vertically is crucial. This is not only because, on a practical level, it will be very difficult to reproduce exactly time and time again an off-vertical hanging line, and gaps and cracks between strips of paper will appear with no hope of correction, but because – rather obviously – most patterns are designed to hang straight

▶ *If you favour a highly co-ordinated look, many wallpapers now come with matching borders and fabrics. It is a good idea, however, to keep the rest of the decoration simple; here the painted floor, plain rugs and understated window treatment provide perfect foils for a 'busy' blue and white wallpaper.*

A few helpful hints

1 Paper in a logical sequence. If there is an obvious focal point, centre your first piece there and work outwards.

2 If there is no focal point, start to the right of the main window and work clockwise around to the door.

3 To match a pattern, lay a strip on the pasting table and place another beside it, lining up the pattern.

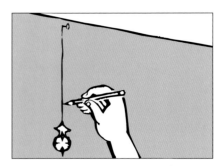

4 It is vital that you establish a true vertical before you start. You can do this with a plumb line or spirit level.

◄ *For those who haven't the time or the confidence to experiment with paint effects, there are now a number of wallpapers on the market that simulate different paint finishes. The subtle stripes of this wallpaper resemble the soft finish achieved by shading, and give a warm, even look to the walls in this smart bedroom.*

Tools and equipment

Tools for papering

- **Tape measure.**
- **Craft knife:** to trim wallpaper.
- **Metal rule/straight edge.**
- **Spirit level:** to check true horizontals and verticals.
- **Pasting brush.**
- **Paper-hanging brush:** to smooth paper into place once it is on the wall.
- **Radiator roller:** to smooth paper into place behind radiators or in awkward corners.
- **Clean household broom:** to hold up paper when applying to the ceiling.
- **Adhesives:** follow the wallpaper manufacturer's instructions. If you have a problem with mould, use a fungicidal paste; you will also need vinyl adhesive if you are overlapping and sticking vinyl wallpaper.
- **Wallpaper trough:** to soak lengths of ready-pasted paper.
- **Plastic bucket:** to mix paste.
- **Pasting table:** any table is suitable, provided it is well covered and at the correct height for you to work at easily.
- **Seam roller:** to smooth the paper seams, once the paper is hung.
- **Wallpaper scissors.**
- **Wooden dowel:** to mix paste.
- **Sponge:** to clean up.
- **Plumb line:** to find a true vertical.

Tools for other wallcoverings

- **Small, sharp scissors and scalpels:** to cut out decoupage motifs.
- **To attach fabric to walls:** staple gun, wooden battens, card to strengthen joins, curtain rods or poles for shirred fabric; mounting track.

and will never look right unless they do. Use a spirit level or plumb line to make sure that the paper is absolutely vertical; do not follow the line of windows or doors as these, particularly in older houses, are not always straight.

To get a true vertical, hang the plumb line by a pin from the top of the wall and mark the line of its fall lightly with chalk or a pencil.

Obviously, it is essential to repeat this process on each wall to be papered rather than assuming anything.

Sequence of papering

There are no set rules about where to start papering; the most important thing is for you to work in a logical sequence around the room. If the room has an obvious focal point, however – a chimney breast in the middle of one wall, for instance – centre the pattern of your first piece of wallpaper on it, and then work outwards from there around the room, in opposite directions, until the two ends meet at the other side, or at a convenient junction – such as a door.

If there is no obvious focal point on which to centre your work, start papering to the right of the main window and work your way in a clockwise motion around the room to the door, before going back to the first drop and working anti-clockwise round to the door. Remember, though, not to use the window frame as a reference for your vertical.

Measuring, cutting and pasting

When you are calculating the number of rolls of wallpaper you will need, it is best to err on the side of generosity and to buy all the paper at the same time, from the same batch.

To work out the number of rolls you need, measure the height of the walls and add 10cm (4in) as an overhang allowance, and the length of the paper's pattern repeat if there is one. This is the length of each drop. Divide the total length of a roll (usually 10m [33ft]) by the length of your drop to discover how many drops you will get from one roll (A).

Measure the distance around the room and divide that figure by the width of a roll (usually 52cm [20½in]) to find out how many drops you will need to paper the room (B).

Then divide the number of drops required to paper the room by how many drops you will get from one roll of wallpaper to calculate the number of rolls (C) you will need to complete the job (B÷A=C). Round up to the next whole roll and add a roll in case your arithmetic is slightly inaccurate.

Time

Hanging wallpaper is time-consuming and should not be hurried. When you are planning the job, overestimate the time needed simply as drying time – after stripping, after lining, after papering – in order not to risk a feeling of frustration creeping in later, which would increase the potential for disaster.

Cutting

Remember always to allow an extra 5cm (2in) at each end of the length of paper for trimming to fit. And always cut before you paste.

Having first established a vertical line on your wall, measure the wall from ceiling to skirting board. Unroll your wallpaper roll on the table and measure out the overall length of a strip, including the overhang allowance. Mark the pasting table itself to avoid measuring each strip. Using a try square, mark a line at right angles to the edge of the strip at the appropriate length and cut straight along the line, using wallpapering scissors.

If you have to match the pattern, cut the first length and then turn the paper right-side up to match the pattern on the adjoining length, before adding on the extra 5cm (2in)

▲ *Highly decorative papers need not be reserved solely for the bedroom – they can also be used to great effect in other parts of the house. This wallpaper in a strong green, printed with a delicate trellis of dew drops and roses, has an old-fashioned charm, and complements the soft lavender panelled walls of the room beyond.*

Calculating the number of rolls

British wallpaper

Wall Height	Distance around room (inc doors and windows)												
	9.1m	10.3m	11.6m	12.8m	14m	15.2m	16.4m	17.7m	18.9m	20.1m	21.3m	22.6m	23.9m
	30ft	34ft	38ft	42ft	46ft	50ft	54ft	58ft	62ft	66ft	70ft	74ft	78ft
2.45m (8ft)	5	5	6	7	7	8	9	9	10	10	11	12	12
2.75m (9ft)	6	6	7	7	8	9	9	10	10	11	12	12	13
3m (10ft)	6	7	8	8	9	10	10	11	12	13	13	14	15

Calculations based on roll measuring 52cm (20½in) x 10.3m (34ft)

US wallpaper

Wall Height	Distance around room (inc doors and windows)												
	9.7m	11m	12.2m	13.4m	14.6m	15.8m	17.1m	18.3m	19.5m	20.7m	21.9m	23.2m	24.4m
	32ft	36ft	40ft	44ft	48ft	52ft	56ft	60ft	64ft	68ft	72ft	76ft	80ft
2.45m (8ft)	8	9	10	11	12	13	14	15	16	17	18	19	20
2.75m (9ft)	9	10	11	12	14	15	16	17	18	19	20	21	22
3m (10ft)	10	11	12	14	15	16	17	19	20	21	22	23	25

Calculations based on roll measuring 45cm (18in) when trimmed x 7.3m (24ft)

Measuring, cutting and pasting

1 Lay the paper out on the table and measure the first length, marking the cut-off point with a pencil.

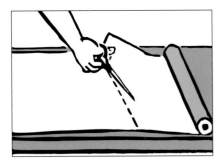

2 Use a pair of long wallpapering scissors to cut off the first strip.

3 Square up one long edge and one short edge with the sides of the table and apply the paste from the centre.

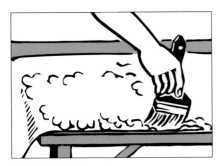

4 Using a wide pasting brush, work the paste outwards to the edges. Make sure the paste is applied evenly.

at each end of the length before you cut across the width. Number each length on the reverse side, in order to avoid any confusion about the order you need to follow to match a pattern accurately when you come to hang the lengths. Mark an arrow on the back of each piece indicating the top on a matching paper, if there is no obvious right way up.

Pasting

First, set up your trestle or pasting table. If possible, position the table so that you will face the light when you are pasting; this will make it easier to identify areas that lack paste – they look dull rather than shiny.

Mix up the paste and lay the paper pattern-side down on the table. Keep the table clean to prevent getting paste on the right side of the paper. Distribute the paste evenly or it will bubble up. Start pasting from the centre and work outwards to the sides, applying the paste with a wide pasting brush.

Check whether the paper requires time for the paste to soak in before it is hung. Leave the paper until it is quite supple before you hang it, but note how long this takes to keep the soaking time constant from length to length to prevent variations in stretching.

Bubbling may have been caused by too much paste. More often, it is the result of not having allowed the paper to soak for long enough; always read the manufacturer's instructions and allow sufficient soaking time. If you need to repair one or two bubbles in a drop, use a sharp craft knife to pierce the bubble. Smear a small amount of paste behind the opening with an artist's paintbrush and use a paper-hanging brush to smooth the paper back into position. Wipe the excess paste away with a damp sponge. This is only practical for a few bubbles; if your paper has a rash of bubbles, the only remedy is to remove the drop and rehang it.

Ready-pasted and foamed vinyls

Ready-pasted vinyl is probably the best paper for an inexperienced decorator, as its tough surface means that it is less likely to tear and stretch as you work. Half-fill a wallpaper trough with water and place it next to the part of the wall where you intend to start

papering. Measure and cut the paper. Roll up the length, with the pattern facing inwards, and immerse the paper fully in the trough.

Follow the manufacturer's instructions on soaking time, then lift up the paper by its top edge with both hands, carefully allowing the water to drain back into the trough. Position the first length on the wall, making sure that it is straight against your vertical guideline (see pages 38–39), and then smooth it with a clean sponge rather than a brush; it helps to absorb some of the excess water.

Some papers and borders are not only ready-pasted, but they do not require soaking either. Their self-adhesive coating becomes exposed as you pull it from the roll and you can stick them directly onto the wall. Further to its advantage, the adhesive takes a while to form a strong bond, so if you make a mistake in hanging, the paper can be repositioned quickly, without a problem.

Hanging ready-pasted vinyls

1 Roll ready-pasted vinyl pattern-side inwards and soak in a wallpaper trough. Unroll and apply directly to the wall.

2 Position the paper so that the patterns are matched and smooth it down with a clean sponge.

Hanging standard lengths

Hanging paper along a smooth run of wall is fairly straightforward, but ensure that you have the paper the right way up. This sounds obvious, but it is easy to make this mistake when dealing with lots of large drops.

Making a concertina

When you have pasted the entire length of your measured length of wallpaper, checking that there are no areas where the paste is thin or dry, take the pasted paper (see pages 40–41) and loop it into a concertina shape, making the folds about 75cm (2ft 6in) long. When you get to the end of the paper, fold it back against itself so that the pasted sides are touching to ensure that this does not stick to the wall as you work your way down.

If you are only working with a short length, fold the ends into the centre, but be careful not to crease it as you go.

Hanging the paper

Hang a length of wallpaper from the top of the wall, brushing it into place and then trimming it to match exactly the join where the wall and ceiling meet. Only after finishing the top do you work your way down to the bottom, brushing that into place and trimming it to fit in the same way.

Leaving a 5cm (2in) overlap to run up onto the ceiling, unfold the top half of the first fold of your concertina and offer up the paper against the top of the wall. Ensure that the side of the paper is vertical, running exactly down the line of the plumb line. Do not forget to check that you have an overlap.

Smooth with a brush, working from the middle of the paper outwards, brushing firmly into the junction between wall and ceiling. Run the rounded edge of the wallpaper scissors along the crease to make a distinct mark.

▶ If you have never attempted wallpapering before, start with a wallpaper that has an uncomplicated pattern, such as these wide stripes. A simple design makes joining the edges a relatively easy task. Stripes, like a plain paper or one with a small, random pattern, do not need matching up so it is simple to cut lengths straight from the roll.

Peel the paper away at the top far enough to reveal the crease you have just made and cut neatly along the line of the crease with your scissors. Smooth the paper back onto the wall with the paper-hanging brush; it should fit the wall neatly now. Wipe off any excess paste, and discard any offcuts too small to use elsewhere, throwing them in the bin to keep wayward paste to a minimum.

Undo the folds one by one as you work gradually downwards, and continue to brush the paper from the centre outwards, being careful not to let the hanging paper crease; if a crease does appear, however, and if the paste is still wet, gently pull the paper away from the wall at the point where the crease has occurred and carefully reposition it. On the other hand, if it is dry, cut open the crease with a sharp craft knife, and proceed as you would to repair a bubble (see pages 40–41).

Do not stick the bottom in place yet. Unfold the last piece at the bottom and repeat the creasing process for the top of the wall to trim the bottom edge. Wipe away any excess paste with a sponge before it dries. Continue to hang lengths of paper along the wall until you reach the corner. Press down

Hanging the first lengths

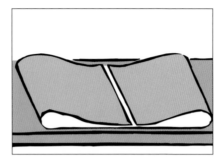

1 Fold over the bottom end of the paper, pasted sides together.

5 Form a crease. Peel the top of the paper away from the wall and trim it before smoothing it back on.

2 For long lengths, loop the paper backwards and forwards into a concertina shape.

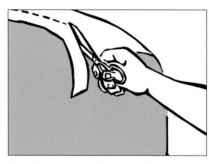

6 Carefully trim the edge of the paper with scissors to ensure a clean finish.

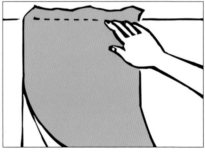

3 Place the top of the paper at the top of the wall, leaving your 5cm (2in) allowance to run up to the ceiling.

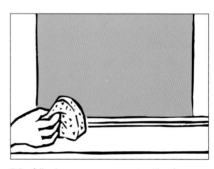

7 Carefully wipe away any excess paste with a clean sponge before it dries.

4 Smooth the paper with a wide brush, working from the centre outwards.

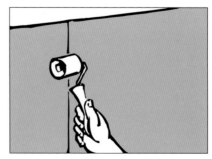

8 Press down the joining edges of the wallpaper using a seam roller.

▲ *Few things look fresher than stripes: their uniform crispness lends them to most rooms in the house. Blue and white are perfect for this nautical-look bedroom, where they combine with a co-ordinating border and fresh paintwork to create a look that is pulled together but calm and unfussy.*

the joining edges using a seam roller. If the seams of paper are pulling away from each other or the wall, the paste has not been spread to the edge of the roll. Lift the edge slightly with a knife and apply a little paste to the edge with an artist's brush. Press smooth again with a seam roller.

If you are using ready-pasted paper, it is advisable to run a small artist's brush loaded with some vinyl glue along the seams of paper as a matter of course. Smooth it into place to create a strong, clean join. And after hanging four full strips, go back over the seams with a seam roller. Check the surface for any paste and remove with a damp sponge. It is always easier to remove adhesive immediately than after it has dried.

Turning corners

When you have worked your way along a wall, you will arrive at a corner. Papering around corners requires taking the paper around the corner edge and overlapping it with a new length of wallpaper, regardless of whether the corner is internal or external. Given that you will be working with two strips from the same length of paper, and creating an overlap, you will inevitably lose some of a pattern repeat. However, a slight loss of pattern match is not always noticeable.

Internal corners

Measure from the edge of the last full width of wallpaper to the corner at the top of the wall, then halfway down, and once more at the bottom. Add 2.5cm (1in) to the longest measurement for the overlap.

If you are using paper with a small pattern or vertical stripes, you should adjust the width of your overlap to the width of the pattern repeat to make it easier to match on the facing wall.

Take a cut length of paper and cut it to this width. Leaving the offcut on the pasting table, paste this narrow strip in place using the standard method, but smoothing the cut edge around the corner. Run a seam roller along the cut edge to ensure it is firmly fixed in place against the wall.

Next take the offcut and paste it. Then, using a plumb line or spirit level, you should establish the vertical on the new wall; it is vital that you do this for each new wall as corners are seldom 'true', or square, and your paper will be hanging well out of true by the time you return to your starting point if you do not – a small problem after four corners can appear rather large!

Finally, taking great care to butt it up right into the corner and ensuring that it is positioned vertically, hang the offcut on the internal wall, matching up the pattern if necessary.

External corners

Smooth the paper up to the edge using the paper-hanging brush and ease it around the corner, this time without brushing it firmly into place. In this instance, you

Internal corners

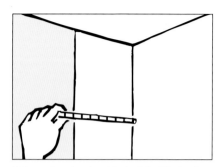

1 Measure from the edge of the last full width of wallpaper to the corner at the top, midway and bottom.

2 Add 2.5cm (1in) to the widest measurement for the overlap and cut out. Paste and smooth around the corner.

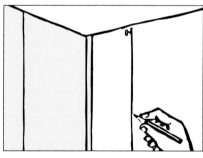

3 Use a plumb line to establish a vertical on the new wall at the width of the offcut.

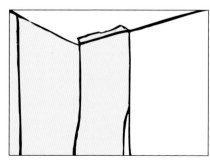

4 Hang the offcut, taking care to position the edge very close to the corner and to match the patterns.

External corners

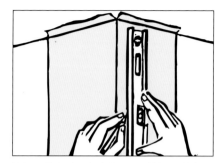

1 Use a spirit level or plumb line to establish a vertical 2.5cm (1in) from the corner. Mark the line with a pencil.

2 Cut along the pencil line with a craft knife, using a straight edge as a guide.

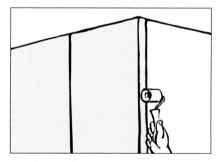

3 Run the seam roller along the edge leading to the corner to fix the paper in place.

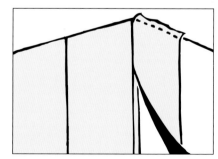

4 Finally, hang the offcut, positioning its edge close to the corner and lining up the pattern if necessary.

◀ *Broad stripes are a good choice for a room with sharp corners. Here a striped wallpaper accentuates the neat angles of the chimney breast, while its muted colours create an air of restrained grandeur, ideal for a formal drawing room.*

▼ *In a heavy-use area such as a hallway, staircase or kitchen, it's sensible to use a wallpaper with a tougher finish, and consequently a longer life. In this case, a hard wearing vinyl has been used below the dado rail and a standard patterned paper above.*

should rub your hand down the angle of the wall to make a firm crease along the paper. Slit the overlap allowance to allow the paper to move around the corner without buckling. Use a plumb line or spirit level to establish a vertical about 2.5cm (1in) from the external corner and use a straight edge or metal rule to mark the line in pencil. Using the straight edge and a sharp craft knife, cut the paper along this line. Gently remove the offcut and place it on the pasting table, pattern-side down.

Run the seam roller down the edge of the paper leading to the corner, ensuring that it is firmly stuck down. Next, if the paste has dried too much, re-paste the offcut and then hang it, positioning its edge very close to the external corner, and taking care to match patterns if necessary. Run the seam roller along the join to try to fix the edge of the paper.

Papering around doors and windows

Once you have mastered basic wallpaper positioning and trimming techniques, it is relatively simple to adapt the techniques to enable you to work successfully around doors and windows.

Doors and windows fitted flush with a wall are relatively easy to paper; the wallpaper merely has to be trimmed back to fit neatly around the architrave or casing. If the door or window is recessed, the increased number of surfaces of the reveal requires more careful fitting – and before that more careful planning. For example, it is important to avoid 'seams' falling on the external corners of the reveal, so establishing and checking the correct starting point before you hang a single strip of wallpaper is very important. All you need to do is adjust your chosen starting point by 5cm (2in) to the right or left as necessary. It is easier to paper the wall with the reveal first, before the rest of the room.

▲ In an irregularly shaped room, wallpaper with a small, regular pattern or a narrow stripe is the best option. In this attic bedroom, the paper extends all the way up to the window in the eves, playing down the room's awkward proportions and creating a sense of harmony.

Flush doors and window frames

When papering along a wall that includes a door or window, you should hang drops until you have one that will overlap the obstacle. Hang this length, letting it fall over the door or window frame. Cut away the excess paper to within 4cm (1½in) of the architrave or window casing and discard the offcut. Then cut diagonally into the paper towards the corner of and as far as the outside of the frame or architrave and smooth the paper with a brush. Press the

paper firmly against the architrave or casing, and form a crease with the rounded edge of a small pair of scissors, before peeling back the tongues of paper and trimming along the creases. Always take particular care when working on the corner as it is really quite easy to tear the paper at this stage. Finally, brush the trimmed edges back into position around the frame.

Recessed windows

When papering around recessed windows hang the first strip of paper to one side, overlapping the window.

Trim and fit at the ceiling level as you would a normal drop, and only then make a horizontal cut at the soffit (the horizontal recess above the window), and another at the window sill, using a sharp craft

Fitting mouldings, sills and recesses

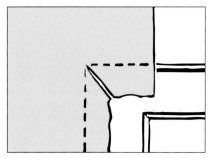

1 To fit a door or window frame: cut away excess paper, leaving a 4cm (1½in) overhang. Cut towards the corner.

2 Form a neat crease around the frame, then peel back the tongues of paper and trim before repositioning.

3 Steps 1–2 also apply for window sills. Take extra care when tackling corners; it's all too easy to tear the paper.

knife. Carefully wrap the paper around the corner into the reveal. Continue to work along the top of the window as if you were papering a flat wall, but using short strips and taking the ends around, under the soffit, to the window frame. Stop when you get to the point when your next strip will be full-length, and turn your attention to beneath the window.

Now hang short lengths from under the sill to the skirting board, using a standard hanging technique. Having hung the same number of short strips as you did above the window, hang another full-length strip that overlaps the reveal. Adopting the same procedure as before, cut the paper horizontally at the soffit and sill, and wrap it neatly around.

Fill in the unpapered spaces in the corners of the soffit with offcuts, matching patterns as best you can. Cut a patch big enough to fit the space with overlap allowances on all four sides.

Crease and trim the paper according to standard practice at the window frame, and tuck in the other edges in turn: firstly under the short strip at the top of the window, and then – rather as you would on a corner – under the wrap-around on the side of the reveal, and finally under the paper on the wall, on the edge that is proud of the recess. Be particularly careful when you lift the corner of the original paper, and add paste before brushing it flat again if the original paste has dried.

▲ *Papering around door frames is not as daunting as you might imagine. This regular fleur-de-lys wallpaper would have been relatively easy to line up. The pattern also helps to draw the eye away from the unusual slope of the walls and complements the handsome walnut furniture.*

Dormer windows

When working in a room with dormer windows your first task will entail deciding which parts of the dormer should be papered – which parts are to be considered walls and which parts ceiling, and thus which sections should be papered and which painted to reflect that differentiation.

Start at a central point beneath the window itself, working out to either side. Hang short strips from the junction of the slope to the floor, creasing and trimming according to standard practice.

You may wish to leave the wedge-shaped walls projecting outward at right angles to the window painted, but if you wish to paper them, these vertical walls should be tackled next. Leave an allowance and take it around the corner; the paper on the sloping roof will butt up to the corner for a neat finish.

Finally you should tackle the sloping roof sections, taking great care to match the drops with those already in place. This may mean that the first length of paper will not be a full-width drop. Below the window, measure outwards from the side of the window to the first seam. Cut to the exact width of your measurement and your drop from top of sloping roof to floor should now align.

It will be neater to tuck the lower edge allowance on the sloping roof section under the top trimmed edge of the half-wall than to trim it, but you could also consider a border at this junction (see pages 52–53).

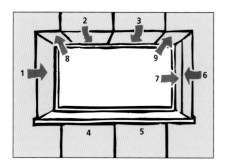

4 *To fit a recessed window: start with an overlapping strip, then hang the longer drops above and below the window.*

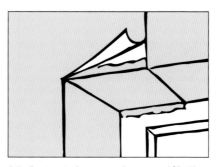

5 *Finally, return to the unpapered recesses and fill with offcuts, tucking the strips beneath the adjoining lengths.*

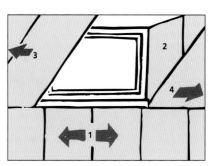

6 *To fit a dormer window: start at a central point beneath the window and work outwards.*

Papering around obstacles

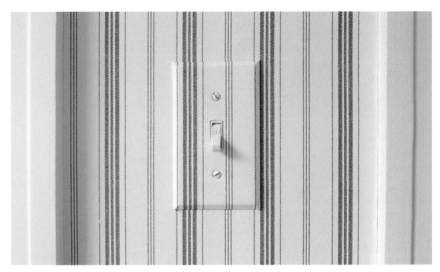

▶ *Papering a wall that has a light switch can be problematic but there are several options. You can paper around the switch, fix a perspex switch plate that allows you to see through to the wallpaper beneath or, as here, carefully match the paper over the plate to create a smooth, seamless look.*

▼ *There is no set technique for wallpapering around a mantel, as each will have its own unique shape and changes of angle. To ensure a neat finish rather than a scrappy, haphazard one, however, always work slowly and methodically, carefully cutting, smoothing and trimming the wallpaper as you go.*

Wall switches and sockets

Before attempting to paper around sockets, switches and any other electrical outlet, always remember to turn off the power at the mains, and allow plenty of time for the paste to dry before you turn it back on again.

Paper over wall switches and outlets and smooth down the wall as usual. Press paper firmly over the edges of the fitting so that it creases. Cut a cross in the paper across the plate, each slit running from corner to corner diagonally. Through this hole, loosen the screws fixing the plate to the wall. Then trim down the flaps of paper to leave an allowance of 1cm (⅜in) all round. Press the paper flat behind the face plate. Tighten the screws again and switch on the power at the mains.

With ceiling rose light sockets, position the paper over the fitting as if you were actually going to paper it into the ceiling. Get an assistant to hold the remaining length of paper against the ceiling with a household broom while you cut a cross in the paper exactly where the fitting needs to fall and pull the pendant through. Trim any excess paper and smooth what remains towards the fitting with a paper-hanging brush. Make a series of small cuts in the paper and use the rounded blade of a pair of small scissors to form a well-defined crease around the fitting. Loosen the plate and press the paper flaps neatly beneath it; secure the plate against

Mantels, radiators and light fittings

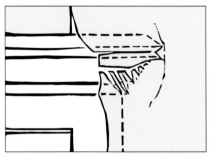

1 To paper around a mantel, work carefully downwards, making new cuts to accommodate each change of angle.

2 Smooth and trim each cut as you go. Smaller and more fiddly cuts may be easier to make with ordinary scissors.

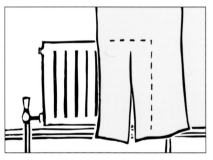

3 To accommodate a radiator bracket, make a cut in the paper to the top of the radiator to form two 'tongues'.

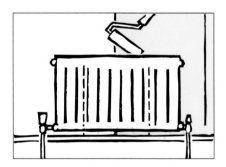

4 Push the two tongues of paper down behind the radiator using a radiator roller.

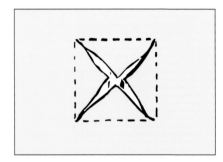

5 To paper over a switch, press the paper over the fitting and crease around the edges. Cut a cross in the paper.

6 Loosen the face plate and trim the paper, leaving a 1cm (⅜in) allowance. Tuck this behind the plate.

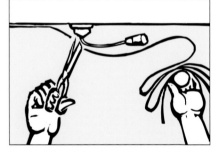

7 Use a similar technique for covering a light fitting by cutting a cross in the paper to pull the pendant through.

8 Make a neat crease around the fitting. Cut v-shaped nicks in the paper and tuck the flaps underneath the plate.

the ceiling. However, do not use this technique with any paper that includes metal in its composition.

Radiator brackets

It is awkward and disruptive to remove central-heating radiators from the wall when you want to paper a room. A better solution, although it can be rather tricky, is to paper around them. Paper the flat uninterrupted wall until you find that the next drop will have to fit behind the radiator.

Measure from the top of the skirting board to the top of the bracket of the radiator, and from the bracket to the edge of the adjoining drop of paper. Remembering to add on the overlap allowance to the vertical measurement and, checking that you are cutting from the bottom and not the top of the paper, make a cut in the paper that will create two 'tongues' in the lower section of your drop; these will accommodate the bracket.

Smooth the wallpaper onto the wall as usual, pushing the two tongues down behind the radiator using a radiator roller. Trim the lower edge at skirting-board level as usual and smooth down with a paperhanging brush.

Fireplace mantels

Some mantelpieces can be quite elaborate, with lots of extra angles to cut around, but the principle is always the same: work slowly and carefully, cutting into the paper up to each change in angle, and then smoothing and trimming each flap in turn against the solid part of the fireplace, working gradually downwards.

It may be, if the mantelpiece of the fireplace is very close to a corner, that you may find it easier to cut the paper carefully across – horizontally – level with the top of the mantelpiece and then to work in two halves. This avoids the risk of tearing a drop of paper, and can, if carefully done, be all but invisible.

You may also find it easier to make the smaller cuts necessary for an accurate professional finish with ordinary scissors rather than their large wallpapering relatives.

Papering ceilings and stairwells

Your primary concern when you come to paper a ceiling or stairwell should be safety. A platform or stepladder can be extremely dangerous when stretching.

It is vital to avoid stretching too far, and important to work at the correct level. This way, you will work more effectively and expend the minimum of effort, thus making a difficult and awkward job less exhausting.

When setting the height of a stepladder or platform, the ceiling should be about 8cm (3¼in) above your head to make the process as easy as possible.

Ceilings

Ceilings are normally painted rather than papered, but if the surface is slightly cracked you may need to cover it with lining paper. Use a heavier grade of paper, as this is easier to work with and less likely to tear than something thinner. To create a safe work platform, ideally you should hire a couple

of sturdy scaffold boards and rest them between two stepladders or trestles. If the boards bend with your weight, reduce the space between the ladders.

First, mark a guideline: measure the width of the paper and subtract 1cm (⅜in). This gives you some leeway to allow for the walls not being exactly square. Mark this width on the ceiling at opposite ends. Stretch a chalk line across the ceiling, from the marks, and snap it quickly against the ceiling to create a guideline. Use the length of this guideline as your cutting length, plus 5cm (2in) at either end (to allow for trimming). If the ceiling is the same width throughout the room, use the first length as your template. Paste the paper and fold into a loose concertina (see pages 42–43).

Position the platform directly beneath the chalk guideline and brush the prepared ceiling with a coat of size ready for the first strip of paper. Hold the concertina against

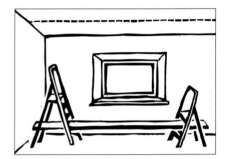

1 Scaffold boards, suspended between stepladders, make a sturdy base for ceiling work.

2 Following a chalk guideline, press, then brush, the concertina of paper onto the ceiling, fold by fold.

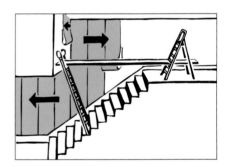

3 When papering a stairwell, position the longest drop first, then work outwards to either side.

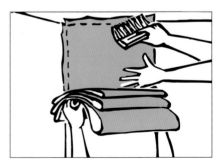

4 Enlist a helper to hold up the folds while you brush the paper against the wall.

▶ *A striped wallpaper makes the most of the sinuous curve of this staircase. A smart rope border adds classical polish and obviates the need for any other detail.*

the ceiling with your left hand or a clean household broom and press the first section of paper against the ceiling with your right hand, aligning it with the guideline. Smooth the paper against the ceiling with a paper-hanging brush, remembering to let the allowance overhang against both the end and the side walls. Release another fold of paper from the broom and work along the guide-line, brushing the paper from the centre out, until you reach the other end of the room. Run the rounded tip of a pair of scissors around the junction of the wall and ceiling to make a firm crease. Pull the overhang away from the wall and trim the allowance with wallpaper scissors. If you are using heavy-grade paper, it may not crease easily so you might have to mark the join with light pencil before peeling back and cutting.

Smooth the paper back against the ceiling to fit neatly before applying a coat of size to the adjoining piece of ceiling to prepare it for the next length of paper. Butt the next roll of paper against the first; run a seam roller over the join to secure it. And continue, using the same method, across the rest of the ceiling. For papering over electrical sockets, see pages 48–49.

Stairwells

Stairwells are even more complicated to paper than ceilings and again require a scaf-fold tower or other sturdy support. You can rent a scaffold tower from a hire shop but, alternatively, you can use a series of ladders, steps and scaffold boards. Lean a ladder against the head wall and set up a stepladder on the landing; place the boards between them to create your platform. You can ensure that everything is completely stable by nailing battens to stair treads to stop ladders from slipping and tying the boards to the ladder steps with rope.

You should start papering with the longest drop. Measure it carefully, and remember to allow for the slope of the stairs; you must measure your drop to below the lowest part of the skirting board and then add the usual trimming allowance. Paste it generously so that it does not dry out as you work, fold the length into a concertina as for ceiling paper

▲ *Here, a soft blue harlequin-patterned wallpaper has been used on the walls, archway and hallway beyond so that the space 'flows' from one area to another. This can be very important in narrow or awkward spaces, where careless combinations of pattern and colour can result in a visually 'disjointed' effect.*

and start at the top of the wall. Because of its length and weight, you will need to enlist a helper to hold the lower half of the paper while you position the top half; if you allow it to hang unsupported, it will stretch.

Archways

Hold a drop of (unpasted) paper to the wall, allowing 5cm (2in) at the top, and make a crease along the line of the arch's curve. Cut the excess paper in a neat curve, following the line of the crease, but at a distance of approx. 5cm (2in) from it. Mark the position of the edge of the paper so that you can then measure and cut further drops of paper like this for the remainder of the arch. Only then should you paste the paper and hang it.

Trim the paper around the curve to approx 2.5cm(1in), and then cut small V-shaped nicks into the allowance at regular intervals so that this turnover lies flat when smoothed onto the underside of the arch.

Paper the wall on the opposite side of the arch in the same way, endeavouring to match the pattern with that on the adjacent wall through the arch.

Then measure the thickness of the wall and carefully cut a strip of paper to this width, with the standard 5cm (2in) added to each end. Paste it from the bottom upwards, and repeat the process up the other side of the arch so that the two strips meet at the top centre. Finally smooth the strip around the curve, overlapping the 'tabs' and creating a smooth finish.

Measuring the stair angle

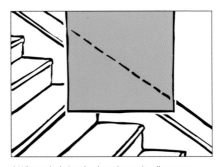

1 When calculating the drops in a stairwell, measure down to the lowest part of the skirting board.

Papering archways

1 Trim, nick and then fold the paper over to fit the curve of the arch. Use two finishing strips to disguise the flaps.

Putting up friezes and borders

▲ *In a room with little or no intrinsic architectural interest, borders and friezes can be used as an eye-catching substitute. In this child's room, a candy-striped paper in mint green and white combined with a cheerful border printed with farmyard animals creates a clean yet lively look, at minimal cost.*

Borders that require ordinary wallpaper paste will not stick onto vinyl wallpapers, so use self-adhesive borders for vinyls and special overlap adhesive to apply ordinary ones.

Applying friezes

To use a frieze to create the effect of a cornice, picture or dado rail, first measure the perimeter of the room at the relevant height where you wish to apply the frieze.

Use a spirit level, straight edge and pencil to draw a straight horizontal line to mark where you wish to apply the bottom edge of the frieze. Lay the frieze pattern-side down in the middle of the pasting table and brush on the paste, ensuring that glue reaches right up to the edges. Fold into a loose concertina and apply to the wall, making sure the bottom edge lines up with your guideline. Smooth into place with a brush.

Mitring and joining borders

Use a spirit level and pencil to mark out the shape of the panel. Cut each piece of border paper approx. 10cm (4in) longer than the exterior dimensions of the panel. Apply paste to the strips of border and then apply them to the wall, ensuring that they run accurately along the guidelines you have drawn with a 5cm (2in) allowance at each end, to overlap with the adjoining strip at the corner.

Looking at the overlapping strips as a frame, take your metal edge and position it diagonally on one corner – running from and to the points of intersection – on the outside

Plain-painted or papered walls can be transformed with the addition of a border or frieze, and most manufacturers now produce ranges that complement their wallpaper. Borders are usually used to frame a feature in the room, such as a door or window, or to create a feature by forming panels on the wall or ceiling, whereas friezes generally come as a pre-cut decorative feature which can be hung at ceiling or picture-rail height.

Applying paper friezes and borders

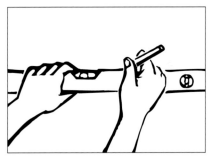

1 Mark a line to denote the base of the frieze using a spirit level, straight edge and pencil.

2 Fold the frieze into a concertina and apply, using the pencil mark as a guide. Smooth into place with a brush.

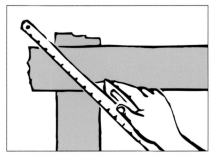

3 To create neat, mitred borders, overlap the two strips and mark a diagonal across.

Fixing a plaster coving

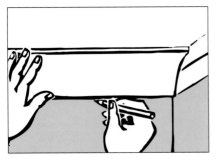

1 Dry-fix the lengths with masonry nails, marking their position with a pencil. Cut extra pieces to fill the gaps.

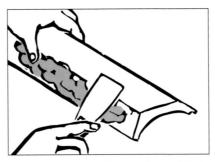

2 When all the pieces have been cut to fit, coat the back edges of the coving with adhesive and press in place.

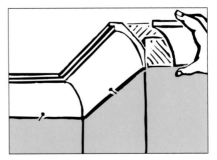

3 Hammer the masonry nails back in to support the coving while the adhesive dries.

and inside edges. Slice diagonally through both layers of paper with a knife to create a mitred corner. Peel off the overlapping border strips and remove the offcut pieces. Smooth the join back together with a brush to create a mitred join.

Authentic period detailing

Using lincrusta panels

Traditionally, these papers were used in panels beneath the dado rail, particularly in hallways or stairwells – sometimes to hide rising damp. Because of the patterned relief surface of these papers, they are ideal for covering cracked walls or for creating a tough surface. Prepare the walls for wallpapering, and cross-line with lining paper (see pages 36–37).

Lincrusta dado panels are bought pre-cut with straight-matching edges so there is no wastage or matching of patterns. Be careful

when you are carrying the panels; avoid bending them as this will craze the surface. Before you apply any adhesive, check that panels from different batches are the same length. Soak the panels in warm water before coating the backs with the recommended adhesive. Pay particular attention to the edges. Align the top edge of the panel with the dado rail and smooth down with a soft cloth. Never use a seam roller to smooth the butt joins as this will flatten the pattern.

Never try to turn panels of embossed papers around internal or external corners unless they are rounded, because the paper will probably crack. Cut the wallcovering to finish at the corner and butt up the lengths.

Cornices and covings

Cornices and covings are fixed at the junction between the walls and the ceiling. A cornice is a projecting ornamental moulding

while a coving is a plain moulding with a concave profile. Both are manufactured as long lengths that can be cut to size. If you fix a small cornice or coving and it looks rather insignificant, you can make it look grander by adding a narrow strip of moulding along the ceiling edge and painting it to match.

Walls and ceiling must be dry and free of dust before starting work. Then dry-fix the full lengths, supporting them on masonry nails top and bottom and marking their position with a pencil. You will have to cut lengths to fit the remaining gaps; use a fine-toothed saw. Allow extra for mitred joins at external corners (the exact measurements will be indicated in the instructions). Use the templates supplied to cut the mitres.

Lightly sand any rough edges, and then, having removed the nail supports, scratch or sand the areas of the wall and ceiling to be covered. Mix up enough adhesive to use in 45 minutes – the length of time it will remain effective – and butter the top and bottom edges of the moulding with a filling knife or trowel.

Press the lengths of moulding firmly in place between the guidelines. Remove excess adhesive with a filling knife and use it to fill in the joints and mitres. It's a good idea to put the masonry nails back in at this stage to support the moulding while the adhesive dries; they can be removed later.

If you are using a heavy moulding, drive nails through the top edge into the ceiling at each end. Punch them below the surface and cover them with adhesive. Smooth all joints with a damp paintbrush.

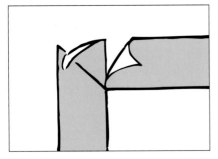

4 Cut across the diagonal through both layers. Peel back the border strips and remove the offcuts.

Applying lincrusta panels

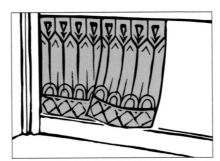

1 Pre-cut with straight-matching edges, lincrusta panels can be lined side by side following a horizontal guideline.

Creating your own papers

▶ *With a little imagination you can achieve stunning effects without spending a lot of money. Here, the motifs from a roll of wallpaper have been cut out and stuck on a curved wall to create a striking frieze of fish swimming round the staircase. Photocopies, old prints and book illustrations could also be used in this way.*

There is such a huge variety of papers and borders on the market that it would be very easy to forget that you can also make your own, tailoring them perfectly to suit your desired scheme and creating an effect that is unique to you. Many of these home-made decorating solutions are extremely inexpensive to create but will not short-change you on style.

As a clever but effective budget solution, nothing is smarter – or cheaper – than basic brown packing paper. Buy it in a large roll from an office stationer; it comes in rolls 50–90cm (20–36in) wide. Apply it to the walls as you would any wallpaper (see pages 42–43). You need to buy quite a heavy-weight paper because otherwise the wallpaper paste may well soak through the surface making the paper difficult to handle.

One way of making one roll of wallpaper go a very long way is by working in decoupage. The rebirth in popularity of decoupage as a craft has led to an adaptation of the technique for use on walls, so you can now dress up plain walls with borders and motifs cut from a floral or pictorial roll.

Alternatively, you could create your own motifs. Look out for strong images that would be suitable for your scheme and photocopy them in black and white or colour; enlarge or decrease them so that they are exactly the right size; and arrange them on the wall – scatter them at random or place them in a regular pattern. Initially, it is best to do this with an adhesive that allows for repositioning, such as spray mount. But when you are happy with the design, stick the images down with wallpaper

paste. You may also wish to finish off the effect and protect it with a coat of matt polyurethane varnish.

Using the same technique, you could create a Georgian-style print room. Black and white copies of prints, complete with all the attendant bow and ribbon motifs, are now widely available, but you could recreate your own with some inexpensive old prints and photocopied motifs. This finish looks particularly good against strong colours such as golden yellow, terracotta or sharp green.

Walls papered with antique maps or nautical charts are equally striking. Use standard wallpaper paste and paper the entire wall in brightly coloured maps, or use them in panels framed with a piece of moulding or even lengths of rope, to create a nautical theme.

◄ Maps can be used to dramatic effect as wall coverings, as shown in this unusual study. Antique maps and nautical charts make striking and original wallpaper and can either be hung in panels or simply papered straight onto the wall with wallpaper paste.

Directory of special finishes

There is no need to limit yourself to paint and paper when deciding what wall-covering you want to surround yourself with. There is a whole range of materials which can be used to wonderful effect. Some of them are expensive; some can be tricky to apply; others require near-perfect wall surfaces to start on, but the striking, unusual effects it is possible to achieve can make all the effort and expense worthwhile.

There are quick, easy and inexpensive alternatives to most of the expensive effects. Would you love to have fabric walls? Are you afraid that it might be too tricky to attempt yourself or that the amount of fabric you would need would make it financially prohibitive? Instead of sophisticated, padded walls, you could choose a less formal look and you could use inexpensive muslin or calico and dye it to suit your scheme. As with all things decorative, it is simply a matter of substituting time, thought and imagination for a limitless budget.

Cork

Available by the roll in a range of natural shades, from light honey to dark brown. Some varieties come with self-adhesive backing. If you are using it in a bathroom or kitchen, seal it with a matt vinyl sealant as it is susceptible to damp.

Flock wallpaper

The wallpaper pattern, often in large repeats, is cut into a velvet pile. Hang as a normal decorative paper but take extra care not to crush the pile with the seam roller.

Foil finish

A metallic-surfaced paper that normally requires cross-lining. It can be used to brighten up and create a sense of space in narrow areas such as hallways. Be aware, however, that it needs a good even wall because its finish serves to highlight any irregularities.   **1**

3

4

Grass or raffia

It is possible to buy luxurious wall-coverings created by attaching woven grass or raffia to a medium to heavy paper backing. With this type of paper, however, it can be difficult to disguise the seams.   **2**

Hessian

This is purchased in the form of wall-paper with a thick paper backing which makes it easy to hang. As with grass or raffia wall-coverings, hessian's coarse texture makes it difficult to hide the seams.   **3**

Cotton

Some cotton can be stuck directly onto the wall, but it is usually prefer-able to attach it by first tacking it to battens or by shirring it (see pages 58–59).

Felt

Felt is available in a wide variety of colours. Because of its fairly dense texture and because it is reasonably hardwearing and does not tend to fray, it is probably one of the easiest fabrics to stick directly onto the wall (see pages 58–59).   **4**

Linen

Some of the more densely woven linens can be stuck directly onto the wall. However, for the less experi-enced decorator, it is probably easier to buy linen in wallpaper form. This is when the fabric is given a medium-weight paper backing to make it much easier to hang.

Silk

A silk wall-covering must surely be the most luxurious of finishes. Woven silk is given a backing of fine paper to create a particularly elegant wallpaper. However, this is not the easiest of papers to hang and it tends to get dirty and soiled rather easily. It is also diffi-cult to disguise the seams.

Using fabric on walls

▶ *Durham quilts in a handsome red and gold stripe make a striking wall covering, adding texture and colour to a traditional interior. Their draught-excluding and sound-proofing qualities make them practical, too.*

Although less usual than paint or paper, there are several advantages to using fabric on walls and ceilings. Like paper, it can cover up minor imperfections in the wall, but also acts as a good heat and sound insulator. With care they can stay fresh far longer than paint or paper. Most fabric finishes can be treated to make them dirt-resistant; later they can be spot-cleaned or vacuumed.

Applying fabric directly to the wall

Many fabrics can be applied directly to the wall but check before you start that they are stain and mildew-resistant. Look out for those with a firm, taut weave that are of medium weight. Felt is a classic choice and comes in a wide variety of strong colours.

The biggest difference between hanging wallpaper and hanging fabric is that with the latter you should apply the adhesive to the wall rather than to the fabric.

Cut the fabric to the required length (plus a trimming allowance), and roll it inwards onto a broom handle for easier handling. Unroll the length onto the wet pasted wall, against a plumbed vertical line, and run a dry paint roller over the surface. To make a seam, overlap adjoining lengths and then cut through both layers with a sharp knife against a straight edge. Having removed the offcuts, smooth back the edges into place.

It is a good idea to conceal the edges of the fabric, which otherwise could fray, with braid or a similar trim. This can be expensive and difficult to remove, so dry-hang several varieties around the walls to make sure you like the effect before you invest.

Some fabrics such as silk, hessian, suede, corduroy and grass cloth are available already backed onto paper to make them easier to hang; in this case the fabric should be treated as paper, so the adhesive is applied to the backing rather than the wall.

Hanging fabric on battens, mounting track and stretch wires

If you are hesitant about sticking fabric directly onto the walls there are several alternatives. The first of these is to fix the fabric onto the walls with a staple gun. The staples can be covered with braid. This is very much a 'quick fix', suitable for rented houses or for short-term solutions. You will get a more professional and elegant finish if you stretch the fabric between wooden battens. Fix the battens along the top and bottom of the wall and attach upright battens along the wall at 2m (6ft) intervals. You may also like to add extra battens in places where you know you will want to hang pictures, or mirrors, in order that you have something behind the fabric into which to fix picture hooks.

For a good, slightly 'upholstered' finish – enhancing the fabric's sound and heat-insulating properties too – you can interline the fabric with bump.

Joining two lengths of fabric and attaching them to a wall sounds complicated but is actually straightforward. It is a technique that is crucial for a professional finish, a variation of which (using only one piece of fabric) is used as the real starting point. Two strips of fabric are placed right sides together over a batten, and a back-tacking strip laid over the top. All the thicknesses are then stapled with a staple gun, and the top layer of fabric brought away from the wall and wrapped over the seam, revealing its right side.

Start by sewing together enough lengths of your fabric to cover one wall – right sides together – allowing for trimming allowances top and bottom, and matching any pattern carefully. Then taking up one vertical edge of your fabric, place it right side down under a back-tacking strip in the corner down the right-hand side of the wall to be covered, as if it would cover the adjacent wall wrong side out. Secure the fabric to the battens by stapling through all the layers.

Take the fabric and wrap it back over the back-tacking strip so that the right side of the fabric is in front of you across the wall. Staple it in place temporarily top and bottom.

Working from the centre upwards and downwards, and gradually outwards, and smoothing firmly as you proceed, staple the fabric firmly in place. Leave a margin all round, then remove the temporary staples and finish off by trimming all edges and covering them with braid. Use quick-drying, non-staining wallpaper adhesive.

If this sounds complex, consider using mounting track to attach the fabric to the walls. This will allow you to attach the taut

Applying fabric to walls

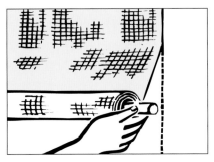

1 Roll the fabric right side inwards around a pole. Unroll onto the pasted wall, following a vertical guideline.

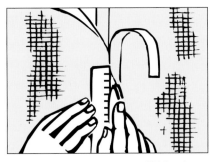

2 For a neat seam, overlap two pieces of fabric and cut through both layers along a straight edge. Remove offcuts.

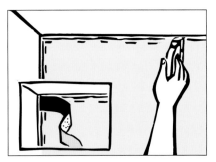

3 Alternatively, secure the fabric in place with a staple gun. Conceal the staples by edging the walls with braid.

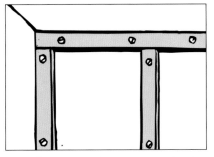

4 For a professional finish, fix wooden battens along the walls at top and bottom and vertically at 2m (6ft) intervals.

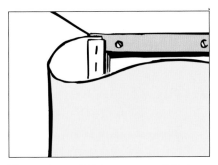

5 Have ready enough fabric to cover one wall. Staple one vertical edge right side down under a back-tacking strip.

6 Working from the centre up and down, staple the fabric across the wall. Trim the edges with braid.

fabric neatly without resorting to battens and staples. It comprises long plastic strips with 'jaws' to hide the rough edges, and adhesive plastic strips to hold the fabric taut.

Alternatively, hang the material from the walls from poles or wires. This is a good alternative if you live in rented accommodation as it does not mark the walls and you can take the fabric with you when you leave.

Lightweight fabrics such as sheers and patterned muslin can be hemmed and shirred onto poles or wires attached just below the ceiling and above the skirting board. You should allow approximately three times the wall's width in fabric to create a rich effect. It can be drawn back over the window or door, or another wire or pole can be fixed immediately above them and the fabric shirred over that.

Heavier fabrics such as linen or wool can be suspended from rods or poles and left to hang freely at the bottom. It can be drawn back over windows or doors, if desired, by using fabric or cord ties.

◄ *Using fabric on walls allows you a great deal of versatility; it is simple to customize it so that it is perfect for your scheme. Here, inexpensive calico is stretched between battens and then stencilled with a bold, gold design.*

Tiles, panels and rails

The selection of tiles available today is, quite simply, dazzling. But before you decide on finish, colour or design, you need to consider your surface. Dainty mosaics may look wonderful, but are unsuitable for the heavy-wear splashback area in the kitchen where a more robust tile might be better. Pretty majolica would look just right in a bathroom but wholly inappropriate inside the back door, where a strong surface that can be wiped down easily would be more practical.

Decoratively, tiles allow you to create many different effects, whether your style is coolly neoclassical or decidedly modern. And having the choice of the best looks is not restricted to those with the biggest purses. You could spend a fortune on hand-painted, hand-made, imported tiles, but equally, you could simply buy a handful of expensive tiles and use them cleverly to transform a run of more ordinary ones. Alternatively, you could arrange inexpensive tiles in an interesting way or use contrasting colours to create striking bands across a wall.

Pictorial panels, relief, mosaic, mirror or glass tiles can all be used in a room of little architectural interest to create dramatic focal points that will draw the eye away from the room's more mundane features. Tiles can also be used to emphasize or exaggerate the dimensions of a room. A strong horizontal band of colour, for example, creates an optical illusion of space – so you might want to think about adding a contrasting border tile when you are tiling a small bathroom. By the same token, an oppressively low ceiling can be made to appear higher by creating vertical stripes of colour on the walls.

Tiling is not a mysterious skill; it simply requires a careful and methodical approach. Indeed, it is a relatively easily mastered technique. Walls are seldom straight, blank surfaces but contain windows, alcoves or doors, and these need to be taken into account before you even start tiling or major difficulties will arise.

For your first project, it is probably a good idea to tackle something modest such as a splashback for a sink. This will allow you to perfect your technique and gain some confidence on a smallish area before embarking on a whole wall.

◀ Tiles are so durable and versatile, it is a shame to restrict them to bathrooms and hallways. Here, a wall of tiles in various shades of blue creates an unusual backdrop for a soft suede sofa. Glass and tiles seem to have an affinity – as proved by the way the glass coffee table beautifully reflects the tiles in its surface.

▲ A delightful combination of textures and materials has been used in this fantasy bathroom. Although the room is small, glass and light combine to add an additional dimension, while the imaginative use of layered wood for panelling adds a back-to-nature feel.

◀ The gentle sheen of brushed metal provides a surprisingly sensuous wall-covering and co-ordinates wonderfully with the textures in the rest of the room.

Directory of wall tiles

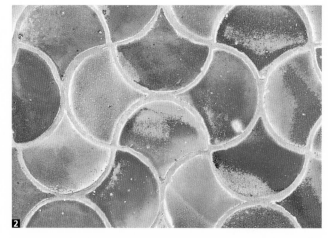

Shapes and sizes

Square and rectangular

Available in a variety of sizes, from tiny mosaic chips to large 30 x 30cm (12 x 12in) tiles. They are generally just over 4mm (⅛in thick). Square ceramic tiles are the most common type, but for variety in a run of basic tiles, arrange them in a diamond or brick-wall design, or mix with the same type in a contrasting colour. Tiles usually have square or bevelled edges; sometimes they are glazed on one or two edges so that you do not have to use edge trim. **1**

Other shapes

Unusually shaped, hexagonal and octagonal tiles can be used to great dramatic effect either by themselves or in combination with square or rectangular tiles. As with any unusual tile design, plot the effect you want to achieve on graph paper before you start on the wall to avoid errors that will be difficult to correct. **2**

Border tiles

There is now a vast range of dado and border tiles on the market; some are patterned, others plain or with a glazed relief design. These can be used to give a striking and professional finish to runs of plain tiles, or a dramatic band between two large expanses of plain flat tiles.

Textured and smooth

You have to consider more than merely the colour and pattern of tiles when you are planning your scheme. The texture and finish of the tiles plays a considerable part in the overall look of the room. The warmth of rustic terracotta goes very well with unbleached muslin, wooden floors and coarse woollen throws. If you prefer a more streamlined effect, glitzy glass tiles can add some sparkle to stark modern schemes.

Glazed/unglazed ceramic

Glazed tiles have a glossy, waterproof surface; unglazed tiles must be sealed for protection. Acrylic varnish gives a durable surface but wax, though more time-consuming and requiring more elbow grease, gives an infinitely more subtle and beautiful finish.

Vitreous glass

Glass tiles or bricks are a great way of breaking up a space without running the risk of blocking out light or creating a closed-in, cramped atmosphere in the room. **3**

Terracotta

The warm, natural and earthy tones of glazed or unglazed terracotta combine wonderfully with the naturally-biased elements of today's interiors. Unglazed terracotta tiles will need sealing with wax or polyurethane varnish to make them stain- and water-resistant. **5**

Mirror

These tiles and sheets can transform a cramped space or an awkwardly shaped room, creating a new sense of spaciousness. They come with a self-adhesive backing, which makes this type of tile particularly easy to install. However, you should bear in mind that you will need a com-pletely flat wall if you want to create a perfect, undistorted reflection, otherwise the effect will be ruined.

Metallic

A less expensive alternative to metal cladding on walls, these shiny tiles can look extremely smart, creating the same sort of reflective effect.

Mosaic

These can be stunning, whether cov-ering a whole expanse of wall or interspersed with plain tiles, perhaps as a border. The small tiles, also called chips, are supplied stuck to a square of paper or netting so that they can be attached in reasonably large quantities to the adhesive before the protective layer is peeled off. Although they are occasionally available in a pattern, they are usually supplied in 30 x 30cm (12 x 12in) plain-coloured squares.

Relief pattern

Ceramic tiles with a raised pattern beneath the glaze provide variety in tone and texture in a long run of tiles. Relief patterns are popular for border tiles and are moulded to resemble cor-nicing for a professional finish.

Pictorial and patterned

Panels of pictorial or patterned tiles can create a stunning focal point on an expanse of wall and need not be expensive if you combine them with a run of co-ordinating plain tiles. **4**

First steps to tiling

The quality of a tiled finish is wholly dependent on good preparation. It is vital to be meticulous with the preparation of the wall and the setting out, because, by the time you get to the end of the wall, what may have started out as a small error can have magnified into a real catastrophe. Once the tiles start to go out of true, there is really no alternative but to take them off and start again.

Calculating quantities of tiles

Working out the number of tiles you will need is quite a straightforward exercise. Assuming you are using square tiles, divide the width of the wall by the width of the tile. This will give you the number of tiles you will need for each row. Then, divide the height of the tile into the total height of the area. This tells you how many tiles will fit down the row. Now multiply the number of

▶ *Small mosaic tiles can be used to cover even large expanses of wall, and are especially good for creating startling geometric designs in bands of contrasting colour, as in this chic, modern bathroom.*

tiles across by the number of tiles down to reach the total number of tiles required. To this figure add a further 5 to 10 per cent to allow for breakages. Buy all the tiles you are going to need at the same time, as you would for wallpaper, as there can be slight variations in tone and finish between different batches.

If you are using unusual shapes or handmade tiles, or will be fixing them in an unusual way, you will need to make yourself a tiling gauge to allow you to estimate quantities accurately. Indeed, this is an invaluable tool whatever the kind of tile you are using.

Making a tiling gauge

A tiling gauge is simple to make and will make your life easier when it comes to deciding on the horizontal and vertical positioning of tiles. It also allows you to know at a glance how many tiles will fit between two points

and ensures that you centre tiles accurately over baths or along windows. Make a tiling gauge from a 1.2m (4ft) length of 50 x 25mm (2 x 1in) wooden batten. On a flat surface, lay out the tiles as you will arrange them on the wall, allowing space between the tiles for tile spacers that eventually will be filled with grout. Use a ballpoint pen to mark clearly on the batten the widths of the tiles and the tile spacer/grouting space.

Preparing surfaces

Careful preparation is the key to successful tiling. You need a smooth, clean, grease- and dust-free surface on which to start. Any imperfections in the wall and skimping at this stage will be magnified once you have fixed a glossy ceramic tile on the top or attempted any kind of geometric design.

When tiling on bare plaster, prepare it carefully as you would for painting (see pages 12–13), ensuring there is no mould or damp. If the wall is in very bad condition you may need to consider skimming it with a new layer of plaster. If you are tiling over new plaster, make sure it is absolutely dry and has been sealed with a proprietary primer-sealer. If you are tiling over a chipboard or plywood surface, seal it with a dilute solution of PVA adhesive first.

Keying paintwork

It is very simple to prepare a painted wall, whether it is coated with a water or oil-based paint. All you need to do is to key, or roughen, the surface of the paint with some coarse sandpaper. Wrap it around a sanding block and it will be easier to hold and use. Keying allows the adhesive to penetrate to the surface of the wall, ensuring the tiles stick to the wall rather than the painted surface.

When you have finished sanding, use a scraper to get rid of any flaking paint and a damp cloth or sponge to remove any dust from the surface. Allow the wall to dry thoroughly before moving to the next stage.

Removing wallpapers

You cannot tile over wallpaper as it is not stable enough. It is necessary to remove all the layers of old wallcovering so that the tile adhesive

Tools and equipment

- **Sandpaper:** a coarse grade, to key (roughen) walls.
- **Silicon carbide paper:** to rub down an existing tiled surface.
- **Spirit level:** to establish true horizontals and verticals.
- **Try square:** to indicate exact right angles.
- **Chalk line:** to mark a straight line over a long wall.
- **Tiling gauge:** to measure long runs of tiles.
- **Length of batten:** to support rows of tiles when they are first fixed to a wall.
- **Felt-tip pen or chinagraph pencil:** to mark the tiles.
- **Tile scorer:** most basic tool used for cutting tiles.
- **Score-and-snap tool:** to cut tiles. Easier and more accurate to use than a tile scorer.
- **Score-and-snap pliers:** to cut tiles.
- **Pincers:** to cut irregular shapes in tiles.
- **Tile file:** to smooth rough edges.
- **Tile saw:** to cut curves in tiles.
- **Suitable tile adhesive:** to fix tiles to wall. Various types are designed for different surfaces or purposes.
- **Pointing trowel:** to apply adhesive to walls.
- **Notched spreader:** to spread adhesive.
- **Plastic spacers or matchsticks:** to space tiles evenly.
- **Suitable grout:** to fill spaces between tiles and make surface waterproof.
- **Wooden dowel:** to smooth and shape surface of grout.
- **Decorating sponge:** to clean down tiles and remove excess grout.
- **Cloth:** to polish surface of tiles when tiling is complete.
- **Silicone sealant and gun:** to fill gaps between tiles and bathroom fittings, to create a waterproof seal.

Equipment to hire
- Electric disc cutter.
- Diamond-tipped cutters.

◀ *Tiles are supremely practical and durable as they are heat and splash resistant, but they can also make a great contribution to the decorative scheme. Here, Mediterranean blue tiles behind the oven and on the floor make a decorative splash and ensure that this kitchen looks stylish rather than merely functional.*

can form a strong bond with the wall surface. For instructions on stripping wallpaper, see pages 36–37. After stripping, make good the wall (see pages 12–13).

Rubbing down old tiles
It is possible – although not recommended – to tile over existing tiles if the surface is sound and smooth. Before fixing your new tiles, roughen the glazed surface with silicon carbide paper in order to provide a key for the adhesive. Then use a slightly damp cloth or sponge to remove any dust from the surface. In some situations, a double layer of tiles may look thick and clumsy. If this is the case, first protect your eyes with plastic goggles and then remove the old tiles using a bolster chisel and club hammer.

Once removed, you will then need to render or replaster the wall before fixing the new tiles, so this will increase the scope of your job enormously.

Tiling plan and preparation

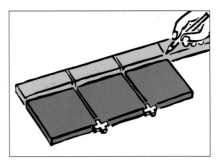

1 Use a ballpoint pen to mark the widths of the tiles and the spacers on the batten to make a tiling gauge.

2 Wearing protective goggles to avoid eye injury, remove the old tiles using a bolster chisel and club hammer.

Planning

Before fixing tiles onto the wall, it is most important to plan where all the tiles will fall – both whole and cut tiles. You can do this using your tiling gauge. If you are planning an elaborate design, work it out on graph paper before attempting to transfer it to the wall.

Setting out

This is the most important stage in tiling, as accuracy here is essential to the overall look of the finished job. First, plan exactly where the whole tiles will be fixed and work out where cut tiles will be the least noticeable. This is a relatively easy task on a blank wall: find the centre of the wall and work out the whole tiles from that point outwards. Most walls, however, contain some kind of obstacle such as a window or door. If this is the case, decide on the room's natural centre point – that is, the point to which your eye is naturally drawn – and start tiling from there. But use your tiling gauge (see pages 64–65) to ensure that you are not going to have ugly slivers of tile in obvious places before you lay your first tile. In most cases you will be tiling to the skirting board or floor and it is unlikely that either of these will be level. It is essential that you establish a true horizontal and tile from that to ensure that each row is level. This is called marking out.

Marking out

Using a batten and spirit level, draw a horizontal line along the wall to be tiled, about three-quarters of a tile's width above the floor

▲ *Hundreds and hundreds of tiny tiles look attractive and professional, but matching them up into even rows can be tedious work. Some brands of tiny tiles are available already plastered onto larger squares to make the task less arduous. The end result achieves the same, very pleasing effect.*

Marking out tiles

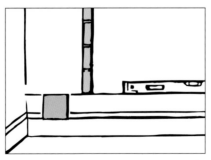

1 Plot a horizontal line no deeper than three-quarters of the depth of the tile. Measure out the tiles with the gauge.

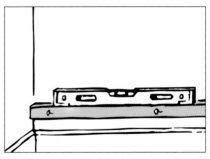

2 To ensure the tiling will be level, fix a horizontal batten to the wall. Check accuracy with the spirit level.

or skirting board. Make sure that at no point is the line more than a tile's width above the finishing level – floor or skirting board. If it is, redraw the line lower down or you will be left with unworkable slivers of tile.

The tiles will need some support while the adhesive dries. Fix a line of battens on the wall with masonry nails, aligning the top of the batten with the pencilled horizontal guideline. Do not fix battens too securely or removing them will be difficult.

Using your tiling gauge, establish where the outer edge of the last whole tile on a wall will be. Mark the wall by snapping a chalk line against it, and fix a vertical batten to the wall, again aligning the inside edge of the batten with the pencilled guideline to mark the edge. Check that the battens form an exact horizontal and vertical before you start tiling.

Setting out tiles

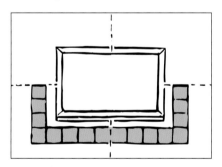

1 To avoid unworkable slivers of tile, the first row should be three-quarters of a tile's width away from the edge.

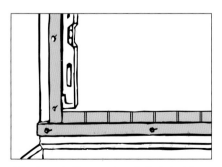

3 Attach a vertical batten to the wall. Check that it is square with the horizontal batten using the spirit level.

▲ *Choosing the right size of tile enables both the curves and straight lines of a room to be emphasized. Tiles are often the first choice for bathroom and shower areas because, once grouted into position, they provide a perfectly waterproof surface that is very easily cleaned – but architects love them because of the design possibilities.*

Fixing whole tiles

Once you have carefully established the horizontal with your batten and are confident that everything is true, you can start tiling.

Fixing tiles

Use the tile adhesive recommended by the manufacturer for the type of tile you have chosen, and spread it out 1 sq m (1 sq yd) at a time with a pointing trowel, ensuring that it is no more than 3mm (⅛in) thick. Start in the corner where the horizontal and vertical battens meet.

Next, take a notched spreader, usually supplied with the adhesive, and distribute the adhesive evenly over the area, but leaving regular ridges. The grooves will create suction when you put the tiles on the wall, thus helping to secure them. If you are using a sealing strip, press this into the adhesive first. If you experience trouble getting it to stay in place, secure it temporarily with a couple of nails.

Press the first tile firmly onto the adhesive, resting it squarely on the tile-support battens. Put a spacer or matchstick against the corner of the tile and place and fix the next tile. Continue to build up horizontal rows in this way, stopping occasionally to check your work by using a spirit level to ensure that the tiles are flush. Wipe any blobs of adhesive from the tiles with a damp cloth.

Having completed the rows of whole tiles, you will need to fill the gaps on the outside edges. To establish where to cut the tiles, take a spare tile and hold it against the previous full tile, glazed side to the wall, so that its outer edge butts up against the adjacent wall. Mark the back of the loose tile with a felt-tip pen or chinagraph pencil at the points at which it meets the fixed tile, and deducting the allowance for the grout that has been made by the tile spacer, use a steel rule to draw straight across the back of the tile.

▶ *Mediterranean tiles in a geometric pattern add colour to any decorative scheme but are also a practical option. In a heavy-wear area, such as below the dado rail in this hallway, the tiles are impervious to bumps, scuff marks and splashes, while providing a colourful point of interest.*

Fixing tiles

1 Use the notched spreader to spread the tile adhesive evenly across the wall, leaving ridges.

2 Position the first tile firmly into the adhesive, resting it squarely on the support battens. Continue adding tiles.

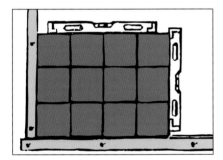

3 Check tiled rows for both horizontal and vertical alignment with the spirit level.

4 Hold a spare tile against the last full tile to find where to cut the final rogue-sized tile so that it fits the wall.

▲ *Plain tiles in a combination of colours can be used to great decorative effect all over your home. In this instance, plain tiles are perfect for this bathroom's understated style and the combination of two colours with white takes the purely functional edge off the room.*

Turning corners

▶ *Tiles can fulfil a variety of functions, as in this bathroom. The stone tile creates a waterproof surface for the shower, while the mosaic tile has a more decorative function, creating a smart dado. The vitreous glass bricks provide essential privacy, while also allowing in the light.*

Firmly score the loose tile with a tile scorer or the wheel cutter of your score-and-snap pliers. Use the pliers to break the tile along the scored line, or snap it against the straight edge of a table or work bench. If you are using a tile-cutting jig, it will have a marking gauge which you can set to the width of the gap before cutting. Do not be tempted, however, to cut all your tiles at once, without measuring gap by gap first, because walls are seldom square and you will waste tiles.

When you need to cut around a more difficult or intricate shape, you should use pincers and bite away a little piece at a time.

Before you fix the cut tile in place, hold it against the gap to check that it fits. If it does, lay it on a flat surface and smooth the cut edge with a tile file. It will probably be necessary to butter the back of the tile with adhesive before fixing it to ensure that it sticks firmly.

Turning corners

Many spaces will require you to tile around corners and across edges. A professional finish here will require a neat and steady hand. Again, when dealing with small pieces of tile,

it is best to apply the adhesive directly onto the back of the tile with a small, notched spreader. This avoids excess adhesive getting onto the rest of the tile.

Internal

At internal corners, you need to overlap one set of cut tiles over another. Work out which edge will be least noticeable when overlapped before you start.

External

When tiling at external corners, you will need to fix an extra batten. This batten should be fixed down the corner, but projecting from one of the walls so that when you fix the last tiles on the other wall, they butt up to the batten. (In effect you are creating an internal corner with the batten.) Then remove the batten and fix the tiles to the adjacent wall so that they butt up closely to the first lot of tiles, with one glazed edge

Cutting tiles

1 Make a score mark across the tile using a tile scorer or the wheel cutter of the score-and-cut tool.

2 Once the tile has been scored it can be snapped apart using the snapping device of the score-and-cut tool.

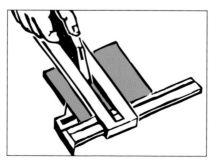

3 On a tile cutting jig there is a marking gauge that you set to the width of the gap before cutting.

4 For cutting round intricate shapes it is best to use pincers, biting away a little bit of tile at a time.

Turning corners

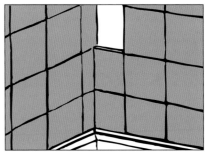

1 For an internal corner, the smaller tiling space should be at the back so that it is least visible.

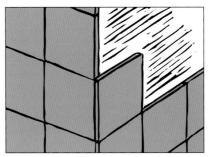

2 For external corners the full-sized tiles on the outside edge should be at right angles to each other.

▲ *No one ever said that tiles had to be square. You can use them as creatively as any other decorative tool, as in this bathroom decorated in citrus-coloured tiles. Abstract mosaic patterns are combined wonderfully here with straight runs of tile.*

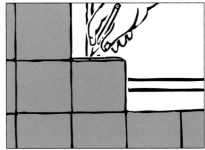

3 For recessed windows place a full tile to the edge and mark the angle which will need to be cut out.

4 When tiling the sill, bring the edge of the closest line of tiles out to butt up flush with the face of the tiled wall.

of the latter tile visible. You may wish to use an edging strip to finish off external corners neatly. If so, you must remember to attach the strip to the corner first before attaching the tiles. They should be fixed to each side of the corner simultaneously so that you can ensure that they are exactly aligned.

Recessed windows

If you are tiling a recessed window but cannot work out how to achieve a neat finish, you should apply and combine the principles you have used for measuring last tiles and for internal and external corners. Tile in rows to within a tile's range of the corner of the window sill and mark the angle which will need to be cut out. Next tile the sill section, bringing the front edge of the closest line of tiles out to butt up flush with the face of the tiled wall – treating it as if it were an external corner. And finally tile the walls of the recess, the junction of the sill and the wall acting as an internal corner.

Tiling around obstacles

Rooms often contain obstacles that are difficult or impossible to move, usually in bathrooms and kitchens, and you must therefore tile around them. Pipes provide a particular challenge for the novice tiler. Make a paper template of the curve you are cutting around and then transfer the pattern to the tile with a felt-tip pen or chinagraph pencil.

To cut around a large curve, such as a waste pipe or basin, cut the paper to the size of the tile. Make a series of parallel cuts in the paper 12mm (½in) apart and then press the paper against the curve of the obstacle. Fold back the paper cuts to mark the line. Draw a line along the series of folds to form a clean curve and cut along the line. Place the template on the tile, glazed side up. Mark the curve on the tile and carefully score along the line with a firm, even stroke.

Place the tile in a vice and cut along the curve using a tile saw. Smooth the edge with a tile file and smear extra adhesive across the back of the tile before fixing to the wall.

For smaller pipes, hold the tile next to the pipe and mark the pipe's exact position on the top and side of the tile. Draw intersecting lines on the tile. Where the lines meet, draw a small circle slightly larger than the diameter of the pipe. Cut the tile in two along the vertical line; score the curve and cut away the tile in the centre of the circle using a tile nibbler. Stick the two pieces of tile on either side of the pipe. To fit tiles around a light switch, hold the tile up against the fixture and mark the position for the

▲ Tiling large areas in one colour is an extremely effective way of creating a feeling of spaciousness. In this instance, beige tiles, relieved with grey details, are co-ordinated with chrome fittings and accessories. The result is a chic yet functional bathroom which makes the most of its natural light.

Obstacles

1 Make cuts in a tile-sized piece of paper. Press it around the obstacle and fold back flaps. Cut along the fold line.

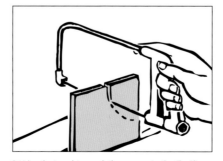

2 Using the template, mark the curve onto the tile. Place the tile in a vice and then cut out the shape with a tile saw.

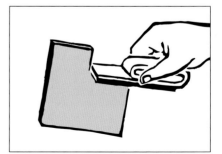

3 Release the tile from the vice and gently smooth down the cut edges using a tile file.

horizontal and vertical cuts with a felt-tip pen or chinagraph pencil. Place in a clamp, and cut down each line with a tile saw. Dab extra adhesive onto the back before securing it.

Finishing off

Many tiles come with a coordinating range of edging tiles. You may wish to incorporate one of these, or to use wooden moulding or plastic trim strips. Wooden mouldings are attached to the wall at the end of the job; plastic strips need to be attached at the beginning, before the tiles. Ceramic coving at the edge of a bath makes a neat, waterproof seal.

Fill in the gaps between the tiles with grout. Allow the adhesive to dry out completely before even thinking about doing this. Follow the manufacturer's instructions as to the drying time; it is usually at least 12 hours and can be as much as 24 hours. Grout can be bought as powder or premixed. Apply with a plastic scraper. Use a waterproof grout and sealant (see below) in areas such as bathrooms and kitchens, where the tiling is likely to come into contact with moisture.

Remember to use waterproof grout for bath and shower surrounds and epoxy grout for work surfaces to keep them germ-free. There are also new stain-resistant grouts available; less likely to pick up dirt, they will thus maintain a fresher appearance for longer.

Force the grout in between the tile joins with the spreader held at right angles to the tile, moving it backwards and forwards as you go. If you scrape off any excess grout quickly,

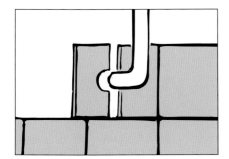

4 To cut out around pipes cut the tile in two along the vertical line. Score the curve and cut away the surplus.

it can be reused. Before the grout dries, take a damp cloth and wipe off excess. Use a piece of wooden dowel to smooth the grout lines into a slightly concave groove, or wipe over the grout to create a flush finish. When the grout has dried out completely, use a clean, lint-free cloth to polish the tiles.

For authenticity, if you are restoring a Victorian interior, you should follow the style of wafer-thin grouting between tiles.

To finish off the gap between a tiled area and another surface, such as a bath or shower tray, use a silicone rubber sealant or caulk. Apply sealant directly from the tube onto the join, cutting the nozzle to match the size of the join. Squeeze on to the join as you would ice a cake, in a smooth, continuous line, with the tube held at a 45-degree angle to the join. Use your finger or the back of a wet teaspoon to smooth the sealant into the join and use a damp sponge to wipe away excess.

Faults and cures

Uneven tiles

Usually caused by not setting the guide battens against the walls correctly before you begin, this is either a disaster, in which case all you can do is remove the tiles and begin again, or you can decide to live with it.

Cracked tiles

If one tile in a row becomes cracked, remove it carefully with a chisel, working from the centre outwards and taking care not to damage the adjacent tiles. Scrape out as much of the adhesive as you can and use a hose vacuum cleaner to remove the dust and debris. Spread adhesive on the back of the replacement tile and press it firmly into the gap. Wipe off excess adhesive with a damp sponge, then allow to dry and re-grout.

Discoloured grout

Depending on time, inclination and the extent of the discolouring, you can either try bleaching the discoloured grout with household bleach, or you will have to rake out the existing grout with a screwdriver and apply fresh. Alternatively, you could paint the grout with a proprietary grout paint.

Finishing off

1 Force the grout between the joints of the tiles with the spreader held at an angle to the tiles.

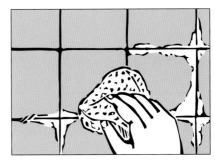

2 Before the grout dries, use a damp cloth to wipe any smears of excess grout from the surface of the tiles.

3 Use a piece of wooden dowel, or similar, to smooth the grout lines into a neat, slightly concave groove.

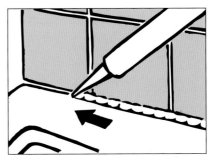

4 Apply sealant onto the join in a smooth, continuous line, cutting the nozzle to match the size of the join.

Wood panelling

▶ *Timber-cladding your walls can be an inexpensive but elegant option, particularly if you choose softwood which can then be given a coat of paint to create a smart, durable surface. It is also the ultimate method of disguising walls that are less than perfect.*

Wood panelling can provide a durable and attractive wall surface that is very relevant for today's texture-rich interiors. You can choose from a vast number of grains and colours, and inexpensive softwoods can be transformed with a coat of paint, varnish or wood stain – either a natural shade or one of the brighter colours now widely available.

An added bonus is that timber is perhaps the best disguise for less-than-perfect walls and is an excellent heat and sound insulator.

When ordering wood, avoid unsightly joins by purchasing lengths which are long enough to stretch from floor to ceiling, or from side to side if you are panelling horizontally.

You will also need to allow time for the wood to acclimatize before you start to work with it. Lay the boards flat on the floor for a couple of weeks *in situ*, so they can get used to the temperature and humidity in your house; move them around every few days to encourage the drying-out process. If you

avoid doing this now, the wood may shrink when it is on the wall and you will be left with ugly gaps between the planks.

Types of wood
The most usual woods used for panelling are softwoods, such as pine; they are inexpensive and take paint or stain treatments well, but if money is no object, talk to your timber merchant about available hardwoods. These can provide a much richer effect, and they

actually improve in appearance as they get older. Some of the more popular hardwoods used for panelling are ramin, oak, mahogany, meranti and cedar. Cedar has a delicious scent which deters moths, so it is often used to line cupboards and drawers too.

Remember to try to look out for wood from ecologically farmed plantations or hunt for old timber in architectural salvage yards to avoid depleting rainforests.

Attaching the boards

To attach the boards to the wall, you will need to create a framework of 2.5 x 5cm (1 x 2in) battens fixed to the wall about 40cm (16in) apart. If you are attaching the boards vertically, the battens need to run horizontally; for horizontal panelling, attach the battens vertically. You need to add a further support strip at ceiling level; but if you are adding a new skirting board, leave the existing one in place beneath the panelling to act

as support. Fix the battens to the wall with masonry nails, or screws and wallplugs, and use your spirit level to check that they really are square.

When you are buying the cladding, look for timber marked TGV (which stands for tongued, grooved and chamfered into a V-joint). This means that the edges are designed simply to slot neatly together when you come to put them on the wall. Alternatively, you could choose something that is a little more decorative; match-boarding, for instance, has a moulding down the edge for a more sophisticated look.

Boards are usually sold in 10cm (4in) widths, but you should estimate on twelve boards to cover a space 1m (39in) wide to allow for overlapping and planing. You can also buy panelling kits, but they are more expensive because they are simpler to fit and come complete with dado rail and skirting board. When you attach the timber, it

is important to leave a small gap to allow the air to circulate freely behind the panelling: as little as 1cm (⅜in) will do. This will prevent the timber from warping and the gap is so small it will not be noticeable when you have finished.

With the framework screwed to the wall, place your first board with its grooved edge in the corner. Nail through its face into the support battens, checking that the strip is straight with a plumb line. Tap subsequent boards in place with a hammer and offcut and fix at regular intervals (spaced according to the weight of the wood) either with nails as above, if to be hidden, or with panel pins as below. Before securing the penultimate board, overlap the last board and cut it to width. Spring the two in place together.

It is a good idea to seal wood finishes with wax or with matt polyurethane varnish when you have finished, to avoid staining, particularly in bathrooms and kitchens.

Attaching wood panelling

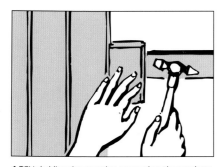

1 TGV cladding slots together as you place the panels up on the wall. Knock them gently so that they abut.

2 Tack panel pins diagonally through the panelling onto the support batten at regular intervals.

3 At a junction with a plain wall, cut the last board to fit, snap last two in place and face nail the last board.

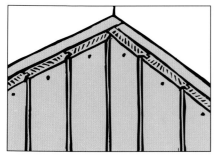

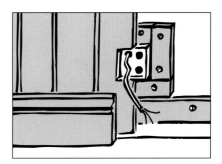

4 Butt join internal corners and either plane a chamfer on the inside edge or neaten with a length of moulding.

5 At external corners plane off tongue to butt square. Finish with dado rail and mouldings, if required.

6 Pack out and remount flush electrical fittings, frame with battening strips, and cut notches in boards to fit.

Detailing for walls

▶ *Rough wooden tongue-and-groove cladding creates an old-fashioned feel in this bathroom. The slightly thicker than usual picture rail attractively finishes off the top of the wooden planks and also has a practical use, as the bathroom mirror hangs from it – the alternative would be to drive in nails and damage the wood.*

Dado rails, picture rails and skirting boards

When fitting a dado or picture rail, begin by deciding on the height at which it is to be fixed. Dado rails are usually placed about one-third of the way up the wall, or 1m (39in) from the floor. Or you can use the height of the chairs in the room as a guide. Picture rails should be fitted at a comfortable distance from both the dado rail and the ceiling, but nearer the latter, and their position should enable you to hang pictures where they can be seen from a seated position. This is unlikely to be less than 1.8m (6ft) from the floor.

Once you are satisfied with the proposed height of the moulding, draw a horizontal guideline with a pencil around the room using a spirit level, or ping a chalk line against each wall of the room in turn.

Fitting new skirting boards may well reveal that the floor is not completely level, but most irregularities can be hidden by lifting the board slightly and covering the resulting gap with carpet and underlay, or by nailing a thin or quarter-circle beading along the base of the skirting so that it touches the floor.

Once the mouldings have been cut to length, drill and countersink screw holes at roughly 60cm (2ft) intervals. Hold the moulding in position along the guideline, and mark the locations of the holes on the walls.

Set aside the moulding, drill into the wall with a masonry bit, and insert plastic plugs that will take 45mm (1¾ in) countersunk

Fixing dado and picture rails

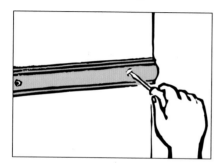

1 Mark position of screws on first, cut length; drill holes and countersinks; secure rail to wall along guideline.

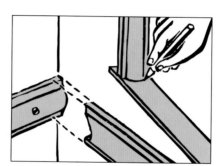

2 For a butt join at an internal corner, scribe rail's profile on back of second length, cut with coping saw and fit.

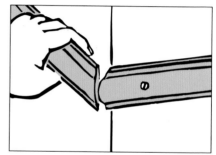

3 Use mitred joints at external corners cutting at 45 degrees; mitre the ends of lengths joining along walls too.

screws. In modern houses, or where layout of an old house has been changed, the walls may be made from stud partitioning and plasterboard. Where this is the case, you will either have to screw into the timber framing, as above, locating this by tapping along the wall and noting where it sounds less hollow, or you will have to use cavity fixings. It is also possible to buy mouldings in kit form with special fixing clips that allow you to slot the rail into place.

Where two lengths of moulding meet at an internal angle, make a butt joint by drawing the profile of the moulding onto the back of the length that will go on the second wall, at the end that is to be fitted into the corner. Cut carefully along the line with a coping saw, then fit the cut end tightly against the face of the rail on the first wall.

At external corners, use a 45-degree mitre block to cut an angled joint between the two lengths. If the moulding will not fit into the block, mark the cutting line on the face, and continue this along the edge at a 45-degree angle. You can do this accurately by using a combination square, or by drawing a square on the edge where one corner joins up with the line on the face, and making a diagonal cutting line from this point to the opposite corner. Follow both cutting lines as you saw through. Mitred cuts should also be made when joining two straight lengths of moulding. Any small gaps in joints can usually be hidden with wood filler.

Sheet metal cladding

One of the most stylish trends of recent years is the use of metal on walls. The trend originated in cafés and restaurants but has since moved into the domestic interior. Metal provides a chic and durable finish, but it is usually costly and requires heavy maintenance to keep it looking up to scratch: most finishes dull easily and show every fingerprint and scuff mark, so they need frequent buffing with a soft cloth to preserve the smart finish.

Depending on the effect you want to create, consider copper, zinc, aluminium or the even more expensive stainless steel. If you think that a whole metal wall will exceed your budget limitations, consider using it in a more limited capacity – in panels or below the dado rail.

Metal comes in sheets or tiles and should be screwed directly onto the plaster, or onto wooden panels. It is a specialized finish and an expensive material, so you may be well advised to seek professional help rather than embarking on the task yourself.

▶ *Polished metal sheets can provide a sophisticated look when combined with other, more traditional materials. This type of room design needs commitment, both stylistically and financially, as it is expensive to achieve and requires a considerable amount of time dedicated to keeping it looking good – every fingermark will show.*

Stockists and suppliers

PAINT

Brats
281 King's Road
London SW3 5EW

Cornelissen & Son Ltd.
105 Great Russell Street
London WC1B 3RY

Crown Berger Europe
P.O. Box 37
Crown House, Darwen
Lancashire BB3 0BG

Dulux
ICI Paints
Wexham Road
Slough
Berkshire SL2 5HD

Farrow & Ball Ltd.
Uddens Trading Estate
Wimborne
Dorset BH21 7NL

J.W. Bollom
13 Theobalds Road
London WC1X 8FN

Nutshell Natural Paints
Hamlyn House
Buckfastleigh
Devon TQ11 0NR

Paint Library
5 Elyston Street
London SW3 3NT

Paint Magic
116 Sheen Road
Surrey TW9 1UR

TILES

British Ceramic Tile Council
Federation House
Station Road
Stoke-on-Trent
Staffordshire ST4 2RT

Corres Mexican Tiles
Unit 1A, Station Road
Hampton Wick
London KT1 4HG

Fired Earth Tiles plc.
Twyford Mill
Oxford Road, Adderbury
Oxon OX17 3HP

Focus Ceramics Ltd.
Unit 4, Hamm Moor Lane
Weybridge Trading Estate
Weybridge
Surrey KT15 2SF

Paris Ceramics Ltd.
583 King's Road
London SW6 2EH

Terra Firma Tiles
70 Chalk Farm Road
London NW1 8NA

Vitruvius
20 Ransome's Dock
35 Parkgate Road
London SW11 4NP

World's End Tiles
Silverthorne Road
London SW8 3HE

WALLPAPER

Cole & Son
142-144 Offord Road
London N1 1NS

Colefax & Fowler
110 Fulham Road
London SW3 6RL

Designers Guild
271 and 277 King's Road
London SW3 5EN

John Oliver
33 Pembridge Road
London W11 3HG

Osborne & Little
304-308 King's Road
London SW3 2HP

AUSTRALIA

Academy Tiles
20 Herbet Street
Artamon
NSW 2064

Architectural & Design Centre
664 Botany Road
Alexandria
NSW 2015

Dulux Australia
McNaughton Road
Clayton
Victoria 3168

Home Hardware
414 Lower Dandenong Road
Braeside
Victoria 3195

McEwans
387–403 Bourke Street
Melbourne
Victoria 3000

Romano Tiles
126 Canterbury Road
Kilsyth
Victoria 3137

NEW ZEALAND

Context Wallcoverings
The Axis Building
1 Cleveland Road
Parnell, Auckland

Levenes
Pacific Plaza
Whangaparoa
and
68 Harris Road
East Tamaki

Swinson Wallcoverings Ltd.
104 Carlton Gore Road
Newmarket
Auckland
and
Level 2, St. Elmo's
Hereford Street
Christchurch
and
15 Tory Street
Wellington

SOUTH AFRICA

Home Warehouse
Johannesburg (Edenvale)
Dick Kemp Street
Meadowdale

Tile City
31–33 Sivewright Avenue
New Doornfontein
Johannesburg

Universal Paints
Randburg
24 Hendrick Verwoerd Drive
Cnr Dalmeny Road
Linden

JAPAN

Loving Design Center
Shinjuku Park Tower
3-7-1, Nishi-Shinjuku
Shinjuku-ku
Tokyo 163-10

Index

Acknowledgments

1 Jan Baldwin (Andrew Mortada); 2–3 Ray Main; 4–5 Mads Mogensen; 6 Simon Kenny/Belle Magazine; 7 *above* Earl Carter/Belle Magazine; 7 *below* Simon Kenny/Belle Magazine; 8 Schoner Wohnen/Camera Press; 9 Verne Fotografie; 10 *above* Hannah Lewis (Sue Parker)/Elle Decoration; 10 *below* Pascal Chevalier (Michel Klein)/Agence Top; 10–11 Paul Ryan/International Interiors; 11 *above* Christopher Drake/Homes & Gardens/Robert Harding Syndication; 11 *below* Paul Ryan/International Interiors; 12 Henry Wilson (Ian Dew)/The Interior Archive; 14 David Churchill/Arcaid; 17 Christophe Dugied/Marie Claire Maison; 18 Henry Wilson (Celia Lyttleton)/The Interior Archive; 19 *left* Henry Wilson (Celia Lyttleton)/The Interior Archive; 19 *right* Jacqui Hurst;

20 Jean-Pierre Godeaut (Designer: Manuel Mestre); 22 Huntley Hedworth/Elizabeth Whiting & Associates; 22–3 Simon Brown/The Interior Archive; 24 Henry Wilson (Giola Rossi)/The Interior Archive; 25 Crown Paints; 26–7 Mads Mogensen; 28 English Stamp Company; 29 Alberto Piovano (Architect: Mariano Boggia)/Arcaid; 30 Schoner Wohnen/Camera Press; 31 Simon McBride; 32 Tim Beddow/The Interior Archive; 33 Jacques Dirand; 34 Henry Bourne (Melissa North)/Elle Decoration; 34–5 *above* Anaglypta Wallcoverings; 34–5 *below* Cole & Son/Michael Dyer Associates; 35 *above* Anna French; 35 *below* David Barrett/Homes & Gardens/Robert Harding Syndication; 36 Christopher Drake/Country Homes & Interiors/Robert Harding Syndication; 38 Sanderson

Design Archive; 39 Ray Main; 40 Sølvi dos Santos 42 *above* Ari Ashley/Interior Archive; 42 *below* Hotze Eisma; 45 *above* & *below* Ian Parry/Abode; 46 Schoner Wohnen/Camera Press; 47 Christopher Drake/Homes & Gardens/Robert Harding Syndication; 48 Paul Ryan/International Interiors; 48 *below* James Merrell/Country Homes & Interiors/Robert Harding Syndication; 50 Jerome Darblay; 51 Laura Ashley; 52 Dolf Straatemeier/V.T. Wonen; 54 Christopher Simon Sykes/The Interior Archive; 55 Mike Parsons; 56 Scott Frances/Esto; 56–7 Homes & Gardens/Robert Harding Syndication; 57 *above* Muraspec Wallcoverings; 57 *below* Henry Wilson (Christopher Davies)/The Interior Archive; 58 Nadia Mackenzie; 59 Lucinda Symons/Country Homes & Interiors/Robert Harding

Syndication; 60 Simon Brown; 61 *above* Henry Wilson (Ian Dew)/The Interior Archive; 61 *below* Dominque Vorillon; 62 *left* & *right* Richard Glover; 62 *below* Paul Warchol; 62–3 Fritz von der Schulenburg (Mimmi O'Connell)/The Interior Archive; 63 Hotze Eisma/V.T. Wonen; 64 Trevor Mein/Belle Magazine; 65 Fritz von der Schulenburg (Paula Navone)/The Interior Archive; 66 Ray Main; 67 Eric Morin; 68 Ray Main; 69 Ross Honeysett (Architect: Ian Moore); 70 Mark Darley/Esto; 71 David Simmonds/Elle Decoration; 72 Simon Kenny/Belle Magazine; 74 James Merrell/Options/Robert Harding Syndication; 76 John Hall; 77 Dominque Vorillon.